ADULT READING SERIES
CHALLENGER 3

COREA
MURPHY

NEW READERS PRESS
Publishing Division of Laubach Literacy
Syracuse, New York

ISBN 0-88336-783-1

© 1985
New Readers Press
Publishing Division of Laubach Literacy
1320 Jamesville Ave., Syracuse, New York 13210

Printed in the United States of America

Designed by Chris Steenwerth
Cover by Chris Steenwerth

Cover photo by Gerard Fritz

20   19 18   17   16

About the Author

Corea Murphy has worked in the field of education since the early 1960s. In addition to classroom and tutorial teaching, Ms. Murphy has developed language arts curriculum guides for public high schools, conducted curriculum and effectiveness workshops, and established an educational program for residents in a drug rehabilitation facility.

Ms. Murphy became interested in creating a reading series for older students when she began working with adults and adolescents in the early 1970s. The **Challenger Adult Reading Series** is the result of her work with these students.

In a very real sense, the students contributed greatly to the development of this reading series. Their enthusiasm for learning to read and their willingness to work hard provided inspiration, and their many helpful suggestions influenced the content of both the student books and the teacher's manuals.

It is to these students that the **Challenger Adult Reading Series** is dedicated with the hope that others who wish to become good readers will find this reading program both helpful and stimulating.

A special note of gratitude is also extended to Kay Koschnick, Christina Jagger, and Mary Hutchison of New Readers Press for their work and support in guiding this series to completion.

Table of Contents

Lesson 1

Review of Long and Short Vowels

ā	ape	gale	gaze	pave	vane	ă	ad	Sam	van	raft	pact
ē	eve	she's	she'd	Steve	Steven	ě	hem	jet	Ted	tense	dense
ī	vine	ivy	wise	wisely	firelight	ĭ	bin	kin	hiss	sift	rinse
ō	owe	dome	dose	mope	cove	ŏ	ox	bop	socks	knot	rotten
ū	Luke	reduce	Ruth	confuse		ŭ	buzz	cuff	cud	rut	putty

Words for Study

Carpenter	dirty	advice	Y.M.C.A.
visits	besides	they're	we'll
window	already	exercise	how's

Steven Takes Some Advice

Steven Carpenter had been driving a van for five years. He liked his job very much; but sometimes the long hours of driving made him feel tense.

Every Thursday night, Steven dropped by his older sister's house for dinner. His sister's name was Ruth. During one of these weekly visits, Ruth watched her brother gaze out the living room window as she rinsed the dirty dinner dishes.

"You're not going to mope around all night again, are you?" asked Ruth.

"Sorry," answered Steven. "I had to drive two hundred and seventy miles over badly paved roads today. I'm so tensed up that I really feel rotten. Maybe I'll go home and try to get a good night's sleep."

"You know, Steve," said Ruth, "you really owe it to yourself to do something besides working all the time. You're still young, but you're already getting into a rut. You should go out more, do things, meet some new people."

Steven wisely kept his mouth shut. There was no point in trying to stop Ruth once she made up her mind to give him advice.

"Look at this," said Ruth, pointing to an ad in the evening paper. "They're starting an exercise class down at the Y.M.C.A. This is just what you need to feel more relaxed."

"Who needs exercise?" Steven said loudly. He was beginning to lose his temper. "I'm as strong as an ox. You're the one who needs to reduce. You go!"

"You don't have to lose your temper just because I'm trying to help you!" Ruth shouted back. "Anyway, this would be a very good way to meet some new people."

Steven said nothing.

At last, Ruth said, "Look, we'll make a pact. You go to the exercise class for six weeks, and I'll try to mind my own business. How's that?"

Steven grinned, "I know you won't be able to keep that pact." As he rose from the couch to get himself another cup of coffee, his whole body felt sore. "You know something?" said Steven. "You're right. I do need exercise. Let me see that ad again."

1 **About the Story.** Answer these questions.

1. What does Steven Carpenter do for a living?

   _____

2. How long has Steven had this job?

   _____

3. What is the name of Steven's sister?

   _____

4. How often does Steven see his sister?

   _____

5. List two reasons why the sister thinks an exercise class would be good for Steven.

   a. _____

   b. _____

6. How does Steven react to his sister's advice at first?

   _____

7. What does Steven decide to do at the end of the story?

   _____

8. Based on how the word is used in this story, what do you think a *pact* is?

   _____

What do you think?

9. Do you think the sister's life is in a rut? (Sentences in this story will help you answer this question.)

_____

_____

10. How old do you think Steven is? (Sentences in this story will help you answer this question.)

_____

_____

2 **The Ending -ing.** Add -ing to these words. Study the examples before you begin.

1. bless	_blessing_	1. bathe	_bathing_	1. bed	_bedding_
2. build	_____	2. line	_____	2. clip	_____
3. clear	_____	3. pave	_____	3. fit	_____
4. dress	_____	4. wire	_____	4. cut	_____
5. stuff	_____	5. come	_____	5. pad	_____
6. wash	_____	6. ice	_____	6. wed	_____

3 **How Do These People Earn a Living?** Match each word at the left with the sentence that best describes the job.

baker
boxer
farmer
fiddler
lawyer
miner
manager
teacher
teller
waiter

_____ 1. This person helps people with their work in school and grades papers.

_____ 2. This person makes pies, rolls, bread, and other good things to eat.

_____ 3. This person plants crops in the spring and mends tools and fences in the winter.

_____ 4. This person plays tunes for people to dance to.

_____ 5. This person seeks gold or brings coal up from the mines.

_____ 6. This person takes people's orders and hopes for big tips.

_____ 7. This person trains for fights by punching bags and doing a lot of roadwork.

_____ 8. This person is a bigwig who tells people what to do and sees that everything runs all right.

_____ 9. This person works in a bank and cashes people's paychecks.

_____ 10. When people are sued, they hire this person to go to court with them.

4 **Compound Words.** Find the two little words in each compound word and put them on the lines to the right.

1. roadwork _____ + _____   6. dishpan _____ + _____

2. sidewalk _____ + _____   7. pigpen _____ + _____

3. toolbox _____ + _____   8. mankind _____ + _____

4. rosebud _____ + _____   9. homemade _____ + _____

5. backfire _____ + _____   10. newspaper _____ + _____

Lesson 2

Review of Consonant Blends and Digraphs: Part 1

ch		sh		st	
chalk	bench	shade	clash	stall	beast
cheat	perch	shark	gosh	stem	breast
chore	porch	shelf	leash	stir	cost
chose	pinch	shook	mash	stone	feast
chow	starch	shorts	rash	stool	mist
chunk	stitch	shove	stash	stunt	paste

Words for Study

peaceful	yoga	difference	entered
Jerome	kitchen	pretty	afford
lowered	wandered	lessons	splurge

Meet Jerome

Steven, who had only his shirt and shorts on, was standing on his head in the middle of his bedroom. His eyes were closed, and his face had a very peaceful look.

"That's a great stunt," said his friend, Jerome, as he walked into the room. "Where did you learn that?"

"It's not a stunt," answered Steven calmly as he lowered himself to the floor. "This is yoga."

By now Jerome was perched on a stool in the kitchen where he was feasting on some beef stew that Steven had made for dinner. "When did you start doing yoga?" shouted Jerome.

"Last Tuesday," answered Steven. "I went down to the Y.M.C.A. to sign up for this exercise class, and I wandered into the yoga class by mistake."

Jerome was confused. "What's the difference between yoga class and exercise class?" he shouted. "If you ask me, it just looks like yoga means you do stranger exercises."

"I guess it does look pretty strange," said Steven. "I'm not sure what the difference is. I missed the talk at the beginning of class. Since it only costs twenty dollars for ten lessons, I decided to give it a try."

Jerome shook his head slowly. "What's the matter?" asked Steven as he entered the kitchen. "Do you think I'm crazy for doing this?" Jerome was Steven's best friend, and he cared very much what Jerome thought about what he did.

"No, I don't think you're crazy," said Jerome. "I just think this is the worst stew I've ever had in my life. It tastes like paste! As long as you're making all these great changes, why don't you learn how to cook?"

"Very funny," said Steven. "Come on, just give me a few minutes to get dressed, and I'll treat you to a steak dinner." Steven really couldn't afford to go around buying steak dinners, but he was so glad that Jerome hadn't laughed at him for taking the yoga class that he decided to splurge.

1 **About the Story.** Answer these questions.

1. What is the name of Steven's best friend?

_____

2. What class is Steven taking at the Y.M.C.A.?

_____

3. How did Steven happen to take this class instead of the one he had planned to take?

_____

4. What does Jerome think the difference is between exercise class and yoga?

_____

5. Why does Steven want to treat his friend to a steak dinner?

_____

6. What clues in this story tell you Jerome has visited Steven before?

_____

_____

2 **Adding -est to Words.** Study the examples. Then add -est to the words in each row.

1. fine + est = _finest_

1. proud + est = _proudest_

2. rude + est = _____

2. short + est = _____

3. nice + est = _____

3. cheap + est = _____

4. late + est = _____

4. great + est = _____

5. ripe + est = _____

5. mean + est = _____

6. sore + est = _____

6. high + est = _____

1. sad + est = _saddest_

2. big + est = _____

3. thin + est = _____

4. dim + est = _____

5. mad + est = _____

6. hot + est = _____

3 **How Do These People Earn a Living?** Match each word at the left with the sentence that best describes the job.

actor
babysitter
bodyguard
carpenter
clown
doctor
fisherman
reporter
scribe
shortstop
tailor
trainer

_____ 1. This person asks questions to get the news.

_____ 2. This person builds and fixes things that are made out of wood.

_____ 3. This person is hired to guard someone's life.

_____ 4. This person learns lines for roles in movies and plays.

_____ 5. This person makes clothes and mends rips and tears.

_____ 6. This person is hired by a mother or father to look after the children.

_____ 7. This person is hired by fighters or teams to get them in shape.

_____ 8. This person wears funny clothes and makes people laugh.

_____ 9. This player is often in on the double play.

_____ 10. This person spends the day on a boat with poles and nets.

_____ 11. In the old days, when most people couldn't write, this person was hired to write letters for them.

_____ 12. You go to this person when you're feeling ill.

4 **Compound Words.** Find the two little words in each compound word and put them on the lines to the right.

1. paycheck _____ + _____

2. toothpaste _____ + _____

3. understand _____ + _____

4. cornstarch _____ + _____

5. chalkboard _____ + _____

6. shortcake _____ + _____

7. classroom _____ + _____

8. undershirt _____ + _____

9. flashlight _____ + _____

10. cookbook _____ + _____

11. workshop _____ + _____

12. handshake _____ + _____

Lesson 3

Review of Consonant Blends: Part 2

bl:	blade	blank	blast	blend	blindly	bloom
br:	brace	bracelet	branch	bribe	broil	brush
cl:	clam	clench	clerk	cliff	clung	clutter
cr:	cramp	crate	crew	crow	crude	crutch
fl:	flap	fleet	flight	flip	flirt	flute
fr:	freshman	fright	frighten	frog	frozen	fruit

Words for Study

health	library	reform	probably
yogurt	Harvey	vowed	suits
yuk	Martin	oh	notice

Jerome Makes a Trip to the Library

The real reason Jerome hadn't said very much to Steven about the yoga class was that he didn't want to say anything until he found out more about yoga. At first he had thought Steven was talking about that stuff he'd seen in an ad on television. According to the ad, if you ate this stuff, you would live to a very old age and always have good health. Then Jerome remembered that the stuff those old men in the ad were eating was called yogurt. Yuk!

After work on Friday, Jerome decided to go to the library and take out a book on yoga. He hadn't been in a library since old Mrs. Harvey had kicked him out of the high school library because all he ever did there was flirt with the girls. This had happened when he was a freshman. He could still hear Mrs. Harvey's voice shouting at him, "Jerome Martin, you're the worst boy I've ever met. If your mother and father have any sense, they will send you to reform school in the morning!"

Jerome didn't end up in reform school, but he vowed he'd never go into another library again. Now here he was, twelve years later, breaking his vow. "Oh, well," he thought, "anything for a friend." For deep down, Jerome thought that yoga was probably something really dumb. However, he would have to know something about yoga if he was going to talk Steven out of going to those yoga classes.

Jerome braced himself and walked into the library. He tried to act as if he went there every day. There were a few kids at one of the tables doing their homework, but that was all. He could remember in full now just how mean Mrs. Harvey had been to him. In fact, he felt so shook up that he almost knocked over the flag by the front door. The three ladies over at the main desk just smiled; but, to Jerome, they all looked just like old Mrs. Harvey. They all wore glasses; they all wore gray suits that looked like something people wore fifty years ago; they all seemed frozen.

It took Jerome about ten minutes to find the book he wanted and sign a library card. Jerome felt so awful by now that he didn't even notice how kind the woman who helped him was. Then, clenching his book, he left the library as fast as he could.

1 About the Story. Answer these questions.

1. How long had it been since Jerome had been in a library?

_____

2. Why had Mrs. Harvey kicked Jerome out of the high school library?

_____

3. Where did Mrs. Harvey think that Jerome belonged?

_____

4. Why did Jerome want to read a book about yoga?

_____

5. At first, what had Jerome thought yoga was?

_____

6. How do the ladies in the library treat Jerome?

_____

7. How do you know that Jerome still hates libraries?

_____

8. Based on how the word is used in this story, what do you think a *vow* is?

_____

9. In one sentence, tell what happened in this story.

_____

_____

2 **Adding -y to Words.** Study the examples. Then add -y to the words in each row.

1. taste + y = _tasty_   1. grouch + y = _grouchy_   1. run + y = _runny_

2. shake + y = _____   2. stuff + y = _____   2. dog + y = _____

3. shade + y = _____   3. boss + y = _____   3. pat + y = _____

4. stone + y = _____   4. rain + y = _____   4. knot + y = _____

5. edge + y = _____   5. squeak + y = _____   5. wool + y = _____

3 **Who Uses What?** Choose the best word at the left to fill in the blank for each sentence.

ashtray
Bible
buggies
charm
flashlight
folder
jet
notebook
oars
punch
sponge
towel

1. A Boy Scout uses a _____ to see in the dark on a camping trip.

2. A boxer uses his best _____ when he fights in the ring.

3. A trainer uses a _____ to wipe the sweat off the boxer after each round.

4. A cigarette smoker uses an _____ for his ashes.

5. A clerk uses a _____ in which to file important papers.

6. A fisherman uses _____ to row his boat back to the dock.

7. A freshman uses a _____ for his homework.

8. A mother uses a _____ to clean up the milk her child has spilled on the floor.

9. A preacher uses the _____ to tell people about God.

10. A witch uses a _____ to cast a spell on somebody.

11. The president uses a _____ to make his trips to see the voters.

12. In the old days, people used horses and _____ to get from their farms to the town.

4 **Compound Words.** Find the two little words in each compound word and put them on the lines to the right.

1. blackboard _____ + _____

2. earring _____ + _____

3. housewife _____ + _____

4. fruitcake _____ + _____

5. overgrown _____ + _____

6. grownup _____ + _____

7. sunlight _____ + _____

8. suitcase _____ + _____

9. eyestrain _____ + _____

10. ringside _____ + _____

11. bobsled _____ + _____

12. freeway _____ + _____

Lesson 4

Review of Consonant Blends: Part 3

gl:	glance	globe	gloom	gloomy	glove	glow
gr:	grace	Greece	Greek	grind	growl	grudge
pl:	plainly	plead	pledge	plenty	plow	plump
pr:	praise	press	prince	prop	proper	pry
sl:	sled	sleet	slept	slid	slouch	slump
str:	strain	strap	stray	streak	stress	strict

Words for Study

dummy	nonsense	complained	throbbing
forgotten	improve	Matthew	highness
phony	sex	healthy	Mansfield

The Phone Call

Jerome let the phone ring eight times before he answered it. "This is Jerome," he said. "Talk!"

"Hi, it's Ginger," said Ginger. "What a rude way to answer the phone, you creep! What took you so long to answer anyway?"

"I'm studying up on yoga," said Jerome.

"Yoga? Isn't that something you eat?" asked Ginger.

"That's yogurt, dummy!" Jerome said. He had forgotten that five hours ago he hadn't known what yoga was either. "Yoga," he explained, "is a way to free yourself from all the phony nonsense that goes on in this world. Some people get into it to find the meaning of life. Some people think it helps them to relax. Some people claim it improves their sex life. I think you should join the class down at the Y.M.C.A. at once."

"That's real funny, Jerome, real funny." How on earth, thought Ginger to herself, could she be so much in love with such a jerk? "Look, Jerome, are you coming over tonight or not?"

"I always come over to your place," complained Jerome. "Why don't you come over here for a change?"

"Because I'm waiting for a call from Matthew, my new manager," Ginger answered. "Anyway, to be truthful, your place looks like a pigpen."

"So, have you got something against farms?" kidded Jerome. "I've always thought the farm was a healthy place to live myself."

"Look, will you stop clowning around!" Ginger screamed. "Are you going to come over tonight or not?"

"Stop screaming!" ordered Jerome as he switched the phone to his other ear.

"I'm not screaming!" screamed Ginger.

Now both of Jerome's ears were throbbing with pain. "Look, I'll tell you what. You calm yourself down, and I'll call back in about an hour when my ears have stopped throbbing."

"You don't think I'm just going to sit around here waiting for His Highness, the great Jerome Martin, to find the time to call poor little Ginger Mansfield, do you? You know, Jerome, you really give me a pain."

"Well," laughed Jerome, "since you call me His Highness, at least it's a royal pain. So you . . . " Jerome couldn't end his sentence because Ginger had hung up.

1 **About the Story.** Answer these questions.

1. What is Jerome doing at the time Ginger calls him up?

   _____

2. Why does Jerome tell Ginger she should take yoga classes?

   _____

3. Why doesn't Jerome want to go over to Ginger's place?

   _____

   _____

4. Give two reasons why Ginger doesn't want to go over to Jerome's place.

   a. _____

   b. _____

5. How does the phone call end?

   _____

6. Why does Ginger scream at Jerome?

   _____

What do you think?

7. Do you think Ginger is going to make up with Jerome soon? Why or why not?

   _____

   _____

2 **Changing the _y_ to _i_.** Study how the first set has been done. Then do the same with the remaining words.

1. grouchy _grouchier_ _grouchiest_

2. rainy _____ _____

3. icy _____ _____

4. stuffy _____ _____

5. bossy _____ _____

6. rosy _____ _____

3 **More Work with the Ending -_y_.** Study the example. Then add -_y_ to the ten words at the left. Match these words with the right sentences.

trash + y = _trashy_

blood + y = _____

hair + y = _____

jump + y = _____

risk + y = _____

salt + y = _____

brain + y = _____

trick + y = _____

puff + y = _____

wood + y = _____

1. A man who needs a shave has a _____ face.

2. A person who is very scared is often _____.

3. The boxer's face was so _____ after the fight that he decided to wear sunglasses.

4. Jumping off a bridge can be very _____.

5. The movie was so _trashy_ that Ginger walked out in the middle of it.

6. Luke was so _____ that he never had to study for a test.

7. Canned soup can be very _____.

8. When you cut your hand with a knife, your hand is _____.

9. The math problems seemed so _____ that June asked her aunt to help her with them.

10. The name of a well-known woodpecker is _____.

4 **Who Uses What?** Choose the best word at the left to fill in the blank for each sentence.

globe
gloves
grill
iron
leash
platter
plow
putty
sails
spices

1. Ruth used an _____ to press the gown she planned to wear to the masked ball.

2. Ted used a _____ when he took his dog for a walk.

3. The cook used the _____ to broil the steaks for the diners.

4. The farmer used a _____ to get the field ready for planting.

5. The housewife used some _____ to make her stew more tasty.

6. The carpenter used some _____ when she fixed the window.

7. The teacher used a _____ to show the class where Cape Cod is.

8. Matthew put on his _____ to wipe the slush from the windows of his car.

9. Mrs. Shell used her best _____ to serve the roast chicken to her dinner guests.

10. The sailors on the *Mayflower* used _____ to get the ship across the ocean.

5 **Compound Words.** Find the two little words in each compound word and write them on the lines to the right.

1. railroad _____ + _____   5. dreamland _____ + _____

2. basketball _____ + _____   6. grandfather _____ + _____

3. underground _____ + _____   7. cheapskate _____ + _____

4. grandmother _____ + _____   8. woodpecker _____ + _____

Word Index: Lessons 1-4

A
actor
ad
advice
afford
already
ape
B
backfire
basketball
bathing
beast
bedding
beginning
bench
besides
bin
blade
blackboard
blank
blast
blend
blessing
blindly
bloody
bloom
bobsled
bop
bossy
Boy Scout
brace
bracelet
brainy
branch
breast
bribe
broil
brush
buggy
building
buzz
C
camping
carpenter
chalk
chalkboard
cheapskate
cheat
chore
chose
chow
chunk
clam
clash
classroom
clearing

clench
clerk
cliff
clipping
clung
clutter
coming
complain
confuse
cornstarch
cost
cove
cramp
crate
crew
crow
crude
crutch
cud
cuff
cutting
D
dense
difference
dirty
dishpan
doggy
dome
dose
dressing
dreamland
dummy
E
earring
edgy
enter
eve
exercise
eyestrain
F
feast
firelight
fisherman
fitting
flap
flashlight
fleet
flight
flip
flirt
flute
forgotten
freeway
freshman
fright
frighten

frog
frozen
fruit
fruitcake
G
gale
gaze
glance
globe
gloom
gloomy
glove
glow
gosh
grace
grandfather
grandmother
Greece
Greek
grill
grind
grouchy
growl
grownup
grudge
H
hairy
handshake
Harvey
health
healthy
hem
highness
hiss
homemade
housewife
how's
I
icing
improve
ivy
J
Jerome
jet
jumpy
K
kin
kitchen
knot
knotty
L
lawyer
leash
lesson

library
lining
lower
Luke
M
mankind
Mansfield
Martin
mash
Matthew
mist
mope
N
newspaper
nonsense
notice
O
oh
overgrown
owe
ox
P
pact
padding
paste
patty
pave
paving
peaceful
perch
phony
pigpen
pinch
plainly
plead
pledge
plenty
plow
plump
porch
praise
press
pretty
prince
probably
prop
proper
pry
puffy
putty
Q
R
raft
railroad

rainy
rash
reduce
reform
reporter
ringside
rinse
risky
roadwork
rosebud
rotten
runny
rut
Ruth
S
sailor
salty
Sam
scarecrow
sex
shade
shady
shaky
shark
she'd
shelf
she's
shook
shortcake
shorts
shove
sidewalk
sift
sled
sleet
slept
slid
slouch
slump
socks
splurge
squeaky
stage fright
stall
starch
stash
stem
Steve
Steven
stir
stitch
stone
stony
stool
strain
strap

stray
streak
stress
strict
stuffing
stuffy
stunt
sue
suit
suitcase
sunglasses
T
tasty
Ted
teller
tense
they're
throb
toolbox
toothpaste
trainer
trashy
tricky
U
underground
undershirt
understand
V
van
vane
vine
visit
vow
W
waiter
wander
washing
wedding
we'll
window
wiring
wise
wisely
woodpecker
woody
woolly
workshop
X
Y
Y.M.C.A.
yoga
yogurt
yuk!
Z

Lesson 5

Review of Consonant Blends: Part 4

dr:	drape	drawn	dreamer	drench	drift	drill		drip	drug
tr:	trace	trance	trend	tribe	troop	trooper		trout	truce
thr:	thread	threat	threaten	thrift	thrifty	throughout			
sc:	scale	scald	scold	scoop	scorch	scour		Scotch	Scott
sk:	skater	sketch	ski	skid	skillful	skinny		skip	skull
sw:	swam	Swede	Sweden	sweep	sweeper	swept		swing	Swiss

Words for Study

hardware	counter	etc.	savings
wrench	concerned	homey	clothing
leaky	family	given	although

Who Is Ginger?

Ginger was the lead singer with a band that played in many well-known clubs throughout the city. She had met Jerome about six months ago in a hardware store. She was buying a monkey wrench to fix a leaky pipe in her bathroom, and he was the clerk behind the counter. As far as Ginger was concerned, it was love at first sight. As for Jerome—well, who knew what went on in his mind?

Ginger lived on the third floor of a three-family house. She paid three hundred dollars a month for her rent and owned hardly anything in the way of couches, chairs, tables, etc. In fact, one of her four rooms had nothing in it at all.

Whenever her mother dropped by to see how Ginger was doing, she would scold her. "Goodness, Ginger, why don't you at least buy some rugs and paint the walls so this place would look a little homey?"

But Ginger would just answer, "Well, you know that I don't make enough money with the band to do anything but pay the rent and buy food. Anyway, it's less work keeping a place clean when you don't own anything."

However, Ginger was not being truthful. She made a lot of money singing with the band and writing songs. She also made a lot of money giving voice lessons to children who wanted to be singers themselves when they grew up.

When Ginger was five years old, her grandmother had given her a piggy bank for her birthday. She had also given Ginger a card on which she had printed: "A penny saved is a penny earned."

Ginger had never forgotten this lesson on thrift. In fact, she still had the piggy bank on the floor in her bedroom. The reason it was on the floor was that Ginger didn't own a dresser.

The piggy bank was only used for small change now. For at twenty-five, which was Ginger's age, she had seventeen thousand dollars in a savings bank, owned quite a lot of land on the east side of town, and had just bought a clothing store in a shopping center. And although Jerome didn't know it, she even owned the hardware store in which he worked.

1 **About the Story.** Answer these questions.

1. How did the name of the story help you understand what you read?

_____

_____

2. How did Ginger Mansfield earn her living?

_____

3. For how long had Ginger known Jerome and where did she meet him?

_____

4. What did Jerome Martin do to earn a living?

_____

5. How did Ginger feel about Jerome?

_____

6. How did Jerome feel about Ginger?

_____

7. What did Ginger's mother think of Ginger's apartment?

_____

8. How was Ginger not being truthful with her mother?

_____

_____

What do you think?

9. How do you think Jerome would feel about Ginger if he knew how much money she had?

_____

2 **The Ending -ly.** Add -ly to the words at the left. Then use these words in the sentences. Study the example before you begin.

✓ late _____*lately*_____

mad _____

truthful _____

peaceful _____

proper _____

wild _____

odd _____

cost _____

shy _____

live _____

1. Because John wasn't dressed _____, the mother of the groom would not allow him to enter the church for the wedding.

2. After the wedding, a little girl _____ asked the bride if she could have her flowers.

3. Ginger did not speak _____ to her mother when she told her she didn't have any money.

4. Ginger was _____ in love with Jerome although she really didn't know why.

5. The boxer swung so _____ in the fourth round that he lost his footing and fell into the ropes.

6. Getting his jeep fixed would have been so _____ that Dave decided it was time to buy a new one.

7. Ted's boss hadn't been feeling well _____*lately*_____, so he went to see the doctor.

8. The fiddler played such _____ tunes that all the dancers were worn out after the first hour.

9. Matthew was sleeping so _____ on the couch that Joan decided not to wake him up.

10. _____ enough, there were more men at the Mother's Day party than there were women.

26   Lesson 5

3 **Words That Mean the Same.** Match each word at the left with the word at the right that means nearly the same thing.

beginning
bright
brink   _____   1. beg
dense   _____   2. edge
edgy   _____   3. jumpy
frighten   _____   4. push
gaze   _____   5. scare
healthy   _____   6. see
notice   _____   7. shiny
plead   _____   8. stare
pledge   _____   9. start
shove   _____   10. thick
                       _____   11. vow
                       _____   12. well

4 **Compound Words.** Find the two little words in each compound word and put them on the lines to the right.

1. toothbrush   _____ + _____   6. billfold   _____ + _____

2. Thanksgiving   _____ + _____   7. snowball   _____ + _____

3. overboard   _____ + _____   8. snapshot   _____ + _____

4. gumdrop   _____ + _____   9. highway   _____ + _____

5. flowerpot   _____ + _____   10. crosswalk   _____ + _____

Lesson 6

Review of Consonant Blends and Digraphs: Part 5

sm:	smack	smear	Smith	smog	smoky	smooth	smoothly	smudge
sn:	snatch	snarl	sneak	sneakers	sneaky	sniff	snowstorm	
sp:	span	spark	speck	sped	speech	spin	spine	spaghetti
scr:	scram	scraper	scratchy	screw	script	scrounge	scruff	
th:	theft	thief	thinner	thirst	thirsty	thorn	thud	thump
wh:	whack	wham	wheeze	whether	whichever	whiff	whim	whine

Words for Study

enjoy	loose	brought	exclaimed
apartment	thus	fingers	oozing
fate	tilted	Tony	rags

A Strange Twist of Fate

Jerome was not a thief, but he did enjoy having sneaky ideas now and then. Right now he was thinking how nice it would be to snatch a can of blue paint from the top shelf to give to Ginger. He didn't have the money just now, but maybe he could pay for the paint out of next week's paycheck.

Jerome had not heard from Ginger for three weeks, and he missed her badly. Maybe this gift of paint would make her come to her senses. It also might be a way to trick Ginger into painting her apartment. "The nerve of her," thought Jerome, "calling my apartment a pigpen! At least I have rugs and books and pictures and armchairs for my friends to sit on when they drop by for a visit."

It was a slow night at the hardware store. "I'll just check to see if this is the right shade of blue," thought Jerome. "No harm in checking." Jerome reached for the five-gallon can of blue paint on the shelf.

What happened next is hard to describe. Through some strange twist of fate, the lid on the can was loose. Thus, when Jerome tilted the can toward him as he brought it down from the shelf, five gallons of blue paint poured all over him, the counter, and the floor. He tried to get the bills and other papers on the counter out of the way, but all he did was smudge them so badly with his blue fingers that nobody would ever be able to read them.

Just then his friend Tony walked in. "Wow, Jerome!" exclaimed Tony. "I knew you were feeling blue about what happened with Ginger, but I had no idea you were feeling this blue." Tony was laughing so hard that he nearly slipped on the paint that was oozing toward the door.

Jerome thought that if he opened his mouth it would be filled with paint, so he just snarled at Tony and pointed wildly at the bathroom where all the rags and mops were kept. Seven hours later Jerome and Tony had wiped up the last of the mess. Jerome didn't know how he would explain the missing bills and papers to his boss. Right now he didn't care. All he wanted to do was crawl into his bed and sleep for three solid days.

1 **About the Story.** Answer these questions.

1. Where does this story take place?

_____

2. What time of day does this story take place?

_____

3. For what two reasons did Jerome think about giving Ginger some blue paint?

a. _____

b. _____

4. Describe what happened when Jerome went to check the can of paint.

_____

_____

5. How did Tony react when he saw what had happened to Jerome?

_____

6. How long did it take Jerome and Tony to clean up the mess from the spilled paint?

_____

What do you think?

7. Do you think Jerome was really going to take the paint?

_____

8. If you were Jerome's boss, what would you say to Jerome when you learned that all the bills and papers on the counter were gone?

_____

2 **More Work with the Ending -ly.** Add -*ly* to the words at the left. Then use these words in the sentences. Study the example before you begin.

✓ fresh   _freshly_

hour   _____

neat   _____

tight   _____

thick   _____

rare   _____

square   _____

successful   _____

mild   _____

certain   _____

1. Sue folded her sweaters and placed them _____ in the dresser.

2. Since the birth of their baby, the Smiths _____ have a chance to go to the movies anymore.

3. The workers stated that if they didn't get a higher

   _____ wage, they would go out on strike next Monday.

4. The workers were _____ in a good mood when they were told that they would get the raise.

5. The smell of _freshly_ baked cupcakes brought the whole family in from the back porch.

6. Matthew looked _____ into his wife's eyes and said, "This time, you're wrong."

7. His wife knew that she was wrong, so she was only

   _____ upset when he did this.

8. Ms. Bond had curled her hair so _____ that she tossed and turned in her sleep all night.

9. Jim spread the jam so _____ on the toast that he could hardly eat it without making a mess.

10. John was able to get up _____ on the water skis on his third try.

3 **Word Opposites.** Match the words at the left with their opposites.

costly
dumb
frozen   _____   1. bald
grownup   _____   2. cheap
hairy   3. child
loose   _____   4. melted
phony   _____   5. often
rarely
risky   _____   6. plump
skinny   _____   7. pretty
tense   _____   8. real
ugly
                        _____   9. relaxed

                        _____   10. safe

                        _____   11. tight

                        _____   12. wise

4 **Compound Words.** Write the two little words that make up each compound word
on the lines to the right.

1. dishrag   _____ + _____   5. overhead   _____ + _____

2. fingernail   _____ + _____   6. drugstore   _____ + _____

3. tailspin   _____ + _____   7. fingerprint _____ + _____

4. anymore   _____ + _____   8. inside   _____ + _____

Lesson 7

Review of Silent Letters

kn:	knack	knapsack	knelt	knight	knob	knickknack
wr:	wrapper	wrapping	wrecker	wren	wring	wrung
gn:	gnash	gnarled	gnat	gnaw	gnawing	gnome
tch:	notch	Butch	bitch	pitch	pitcher	watchman
dge:	ledge	lodge	judge	nudge	trudge	ridge
gh and ght:	lighten	tighten	tightly	mighty	sigh	slight

Words for Study

involved	force	nearby	unhealthy
afterward	nasty	sugar	dentist
Holly	you've	restless	practice

At Yoga Class

Steven had a slight cold, but he decided to go to his yoga class anyway. He glanced at his wristwatch and saw that he would have to leave right away if he was going to get there by eight o'clock.

Once he was in class, Steven became so involved in the new exercises they were learning that he forgot all about his cold. He was getting the knack of these exercises more quickly than he ever had before. Who knew? Maybe some day he would become a yoga teacher.

Afterward Holly, who worked out on the mat next to Steven, asked him if he wanted to go out for a cup of coffee. "Sure," said Steven between sneezes, "why not?" It seemed that the minute class ended, his cold came back in full force.

"That's a nasty cold you've got, Steve. Are you doing anything to get rid of it?" asked Holly as they sat down at the counter in a nearby coffee shop.

"No, I'll be all right," answered Steven.

"You know, I should lend you this book I have about yoga," said Holly. "It tells how yoga isn't just a matter of doing exercises. You also have to eat certain foods and change other parts of your life. Yoga is a whole way of life. The book says that if you do these certain things, you never get sick or feel as if you're under a lot of stress."

"What does the book say about chocolate cake?" laughed Steven, who had decided to order a slice.

"Chocolate cake is awful for you!" exclaimed Holly.

"Oh, come on, Holly. One little slice of chocolate cake?" asked Steven.

"It's the sugar," Holly explained. "The book says sugar is one of the worst things in the world for you. It's a main cause of feeling grouchy and restless. It's also one of the main reasons why so many people are fat and unhealthy."

"You sound just like my dentist," laughed Steven, "and he doesn't even practice yoga." Then Steven sighed and said, "Well, so much for chocolate cake." He was beginning to see that getting involved with yoga was like so many other things in life: there was more to think about than he thought there would be.

1 **About the Story.** Answer these questions.

1. How did Steven feel just before he left for his yoga class?

_____

2. Why did Steven think that some day he might become a yoga teacher?

_____

3. What did Holly ask Steven when the yoga class was over?

_____

4. What did Holly think was so awful about chocolate cake?

_____

5. Does Steven order a slice of chocolate cake? How do you know?

_____

_____

6. What did Steven learn about yoga from talking to Holly?

_____

7. This story takes place in three places. Name them in order.

    a. _____

    b. _____

    c. _____

2 The Endings -ful and -less.

A. Study the example and then add -ful or -less to the words.

rest + less   _restless_

stress + ful   _____

sugar + less   _____

spot + less   _____

arm + ful   _____

peace + ful   _____

harm + ful   _____

taste + less   _____

B. Study the example and then match each word you wrote with the sentence that best describes it.

_____ 1. This word describes a feeling of strain on the nerves.

_____ 2. This word describes how some people feel about food that has not been salted.

_____ 3. This word describes what Holly and Steven's dentist thought sugar was.

_____ 4. This word describes a huge load that a person is carrying.

_____ 5. This word describes a person who feels very calm inside.

restless 6. This word describes a person who has trouble relaxing.

_____ 7. This word describes a room that is really clean.

_____ 8. This word describes the kind of chewing gum that Holly would chew.

3 **Same or Opposite?** If the pair of words means nearly the same thing, write *same* on the line to the right. If the pair of words doesn't mean the same thing at all, write *opposite* on the line.

1. ceiling   floor   _____

2. gloom   joy   _____

3. idea   thought   _____

4. nearby   close   _____

5. penny   cent   _____

6. queer   odd   _____

7. raise   lower   _____

8. scour   scrub   _____

9. slang   proper speech _____

10. smear   smudge   _____

11. stood   knelt   _____

12. vowels   *a, e, i, o, u*   _____

4 **Compound Words.** Find the two little words in each compound word and put them on the lines to the right.

1. knockout   _____ + _____   6. doorknob   _____ + _____

2. shipwreck _____ + _____   7. restroom   _____ + _____

3. lifeguard _____ + _____   8. comeback   _____ + _____

4. matchbook _____ + _____   9. eyesight   _____ + _____

5. lighthouse _____ + _____   10. kneecap   _____ + _____

Lesson 8

Review of Vowel Combinations: Part 1

ai:	aim	bait	braid	faith	Gail	grain	mailbox	waist
ee:	breeze	geese	greet	greedy	Lee	tee	teepee	
ēa:	bead	leap	flea	plea	pleased	veal	grease	season
ĕa:	dread	dreadful	tread	weather	feather	leather		
ui:	fruit	grapefruit	bruise	cruise	cruiser	juice	juicy	

Words for Study

softly	mailman	moments	bragging
folks	route	yeah	who's
agreed	expect	happiness	daily

Ginger Gives Some Advice

Gail slouched against the doorway of Ginger's apartment with a leather suitcase in her hand. There were bruises on her face, and she was crying softly.

"Gail!" cried Ginger. "What on earth happened? You look awful!"

"I don't want to put you to any trouble," sighed Gail as she put her suitcase down, "but is it okay if I stay here for a day or two? I hate to be by myself when I'm feeling like this."

"Sure," answered Ginger, "of course, it's all right. You want some grapefruit? I was just making breakfast. Tell me what happened."

"Skip the food. I'll just have some coffee. I'm too upset to eat anything," cried Gail.

"Gail, will you just sit down and tell me what happened?" pleaded Ginger.

"Well," Gail began, "I dropped by to see my folks. I wanted to ask them if they could lend me the money for a down payment on a new car. My father lost his temper and started complaining that the only time I ever visited them was when I needed some money. I started yelling, and the next thing I knew, my father told me not to come back until I learned to care more about human happiness than greed."

"So, how did you get those bruises?" asked Ginger. "Your father didn't hit you, did he?"

Gail shook her head. "No. I was so angry that, when I left, I banged my head against the front door. I don't think he even cared whether or not I was hurt. Oh, Ginger, it was just dreadful!"

"It sounds dreadful," agreed Ginger. "You know you do only go over there when you want money, and you should know by now how your father gets whenever the question of money comes up. When are you going to learn?"

Gail was really crying now. "He thinks he's such a big shot. Always bragging about how strong he is. A flea could knock him over. All he is is an old mailman who walks the same route day after day, year after year."

"What on earth has his job got to do with anything?" asked Ginger. "You know very well your father's proud of his job, and the fact that you're always putting him down for it doesn't help matters any. What do you expect him to do—kiss and hug you for calling him a dumb mailman who couldn't hurt a flea?"

Gail stared at Ginger for a few moments and then said slowly, "You know, Ginger, I never thought of it that way."

Ginger just said, "Yeah, well there are a lot of things you better start thinking about. Now go wash your face, and I'll fix you some breakfast."

1 **About the Story.** Answer these questions.

1. Where does this story take place?

_____

2. What time of day do you think the story takes place? Why did you choose this time?

_____

3. What did Gail want from Ginger?

_____

4. Why was Gail's father so angry with her?

_____

5. Why was Gail's face so bruised?

_____

6. What advice did Ginger give Gail?

_____

7. Does Gail live with her parents? How do you know?

_____

_____

What do you think?

8. Do you agree with Ginger's advice? (Be sure to explain your answer.)

_____

2 More Work with the Endings -ful and -less.

A. Study the example and then add -ful or -less to the words.

count + less   _countless_

faith + ful   _____

home + less   _____

joy + ful   _____

pain + ful   _____

pain + less   _____

spoon + ful   _____

sun + less   _____

watch + ful   _____

worth + less   _____

B. Study the example and then match each word you wrote with the sentence that best describes it.

_____ 1. This word describes a family that doesn't have a place to live.

_____ 2. This is as much as a spoon will hold.

_____ 3. This word describes a gloomy day when there is hardly any sunlight.

_____ 4. This is another word to describe a person who is loyal.

_____ 5. This word describes something that hurts you very much.

_____ 6. This word describes a person who doesn't miss a trick because his eyes are always open.

_____ 7. This word describes a feeling of great happiness.

___countless___ 8. This word describes something that happens so many times that it's hard to keep track of the number.

_____ 9. This word describes something that doesn't hurt you at all.

_____ 10. This word describes something that would bring a person very little money if he tried to sell it.

3 **Same or Opposite?** If the pair of words means nearly the same thing, write *same* on the line to the right. If the pair of words doesn't mean the same thing at all, write *opposite* on the line.

1. afterward   before   _____

2. aim   goal   _____

3. cluttered   messy   _____

4. dreadful   awful   _____

5. joyful   gloomy   _____

6. lively   dull   _____

7. mighty   strong   _____

8. nasty   kind   _____

9. nudge   poke   _____

10. pitcher   catcher   _____

11. pleased   troubled   _____

12. snarl   growl   _____

4 **Compound Words.** To find the answers, choose a word from **List A** and add a word from **List B** to it. Study the example before you begin.

List A   **List B**

cheap   baby
✓ coffee   balls
cry   board
kin   ✓ cake
leap   cloth
meat   folks
news   fork
pitch   frog
score   line
spend   skate
waist   stand
wash   thrift

coffeecake   1. This is a kind of cake or roll that is often coated with nuts and sugar.

_____   2. Many people stop here to buy the daily paper.

_____   3. You use this when you take a bath.

_____   4. Many people like to eat these with spaghetti.

_____   5. The fans glance at this to see who's winning the game.

_____   6. Many people watch what they eat to keep this part of their bodies looking slim.

_____   7. In this game, you jump over the back of the person in front of you.

_____   8. Farmers and others use this tool for tossing hay and straw.

_____   9. This person whines and complains when he doesn't get his own way.

_____   10. These people are related to you by birth.

_____   11. This person refuses to spend money unless he really has to.

_____   12. This person has a lot of trouble saving money. He wants to spend it all!

A
actor
ad
advice
afford
afterward
agree
aim
already
although
anymore
apartment
ape
armful

B
backfire
bait
basketball
bathing
bead
beast
bedding
beginning
bench
besides
billfold
bin
bitch
blackboard
blade
blank
blast
blend
blessing
blindly
bloody
bloom
bobsled
bop
bossy
Boy Scout
brace
bracelet
brag
braid
brainy
branch
breast
breeze
bribe
broil
brought
bruise
brush
buggy
building

Butch
buzz

C
camping
carpenter
certainly
chalk
chalkboard
cheapskate
cheat
chore
chose
chow
chunk
clam
clash
classroom
clearing
clench
clerk
cliff
clipping
clothing
clung
clutter
coffeecake
comeback
coming
complain
concern
confuse
cornstarch
cost
costly
counter
countless
cove
cramp
crate
crew
crosswalk
crow
crude
cruise
cruiser
crutch
crybaby
cud
cuff
cutting

D
daily
dense
dentist
difference
dirty

dishpan
dishrag
doggy
dome
doorknob
dose
drape
drawn
dread
dreadful
dreamer
dreamland
drench
dressing
drift
drill
drip
drug
drugstore
dummy

E
earring
edgy
enjoy
enter
etc.
eve
exclaim
exercise
expect
eyesight
eyestrain

F
faith
faithful
family
fate
feast
feather
finger
fingernail
fingerprint
firelight
fisherman
fitting
flap
flashlight
flea
fleet
flight
flip
flirt
flowerpot
flute
folk(s)
footing
force

forgotten
freeway
freshly
freshman
fright
frighten
frog
frozen
fruit
fruitcake

G
Gail
gale
gaze
geese
given
glance
globe
gloom
gloomy
glove
glow
gnarled
gnash
gnat
gnaw
gnawing
gnome
gosh
grace
grain
grandfather
grandmother
grapefruit
grease
Greece
greedy
Greek
greet
grill
grind
grouchy
growl
grownup
grudge
gumdrop

H
hairy
handshake
happiness
hardware
Harvey
health
healthy
hem
highness

highway
hiss
Holly
homemade
homey
hourly
housewife
how's

I
icing
improve
inside
involve
ivy

J
Jerome
jet
joyful
judge
juice
juicy
jumpy

K
kin
kinfolk(s)
kitchen
knack
knapsack
kneecap
knelt
knickknack
knight
knob
knockout
knot
knotty

L
lately
lawyer
leaky
leap
leapfrog
leash
leather
ledge
Lee
lesson
library
lifeguard
lighten
lighthouse
lining
lively
lodge
loose

lower
Luke

M
madly
mailbox
mailman
mankind
Mansfield
Martin
mash
matchbook
Matthew
meatball
mighty
mildly
mist
moment
mope

N
nasty
nearby
neatly
newspaper
newsstand
nonsense
notch
notice
nudge

O
oddly
oh
ooze
overboard
overgrown
overhead
owe
ox

P
pact
padding
painful
painless
paste
patty
pave
paving
peaceful
peacefully
peeler
perch
phony
pigpen
pinch
pitch
pitcher
pitchfork
plainly

plea
plead
pleased
pledge
plenty
plow
plump
porch
practice
praise
press
pretty
prince
probably
prop
proper
properly
pry
puffy
putty

Q

R
raft
rag
railroad
rainy
rarely
rash
reduce
reform
reporter
restless
restroom
ridge
ringside
rinse
risky
roadwork
rosebud
rotten
route
runny
rut
Ruth

S
sailor
salty
Sam
savings
scale
scald
scarecrow
scold
scoop
scorch

scoreboard
Scotch
Scott
scour
scram
scraper
scratchy
screw
script
scrounge
scruff
season
sex
shade
shady
shaky
shark
she'd
shelf
she's
shipwreck
shook
shopping
shortcake
shorts
shove
shyly
sidewalk
sift
sigh
skater
sketch
ski
skid
skillful
skinny

skip
skull
sled
sleet
slept
slid
slight
slouch
slump
smack
smear
Smith
smog
smoky
smooth
smoothly
smudge
snapshot
snarl
snatch
sneak
sneakers
sneaky
sniff
snowball
snowstorm
socks
softly
spaghetti
span
spark
speck
sped
speech
spendthrift
spin

spine
splurge
spoonful
spotless
squarely
squeaky
stage fright
stall
starch
stash
stem
Steve
Steven
stir
stitch
stone
stony
stool
strain
strap
stray
streak
stress
stressful
strict
stuffing
stuffy
stunt
successfully
sue
sugar
sugarless
suit
suitcase
sunglasses
sunless

swam
Swede
Sweden
sweep
sweeper
swept
swing
Swiss

T
tailspin
tasteless
tasty
Ted
tee
teepee
teller
tense
Thanksgiving
theft
they're
thickly
thief
thinner
thirst
thirsty
thorn
thread
threat
threaten
thrift
thrifty
throb
throughout
thud
thump
thus

tighten
tightly
tilt
Tony
toolbox
toothbrush
toothpaste
trace
trainer
trance
trashy
tread
trend
tribe
tricky
troop
trooper
trout
truce
trudge
truthfully
U
underground
undershirt
understand
unhealthy
V
van
vane
veal
vine
visit
vow
W
waist
waistline

waiter
wander
washcloth
washing
watchful
watchman
weather
wedding
we'll
whack
wham
wheeze
whether
whichever
whiff
whim
whine
who's
wildly
window
wiring
wise
wisely
woodpecker
woody
woolly
workshop
worthless
wrapper
wrapping
wrecker
wren
wrench
wring
wrung
X

Y
yeah
Y.M.C.A.
yoga
yogurt
you've
yuk!
Z

Lesson 9

Review of Vowel Combinations: Part 2

oa:	boast	moan	oak	oats	oatmeal	poach	throat
oo:	boom	booty	goof	roof	moose	noose	stoop
oo:	brook	nook	woodwork	bookworm	bookcase	bookshelf	
ou:	pout	pounce	trounce	bound	spout	sprout	trousers
oi:	moist	hoist	toil	boiler	void	avoid	rejoice
oy:	Joyce	loyally	loyalty	royally	royalty	ahoy	

Words for Study

lousy	pleasant	you'll	brownies
huh	forgive	invited	sample
how's	forgiven	sandwiches	quarter

A Phone Call from a Friend

It had now been four weeks since Jerome had seen Ginger. Of course, he could have called her up, but that would have been against his rules on how to treat women. Jerome felt so lousy that he thought maybe he'd drive downtown and have a drink even though he avoided noisy bars as often as he could.

Jerome was a bookworm who often liked to read himself out of his bad moods, but he had already read every book on his bookshelf at least twice. Besides, he didn't think that even reading could help him tonight. He was too down in the dumps.

Jerome was tucking his trousers into his boots when the phone rang. "It's Ginger!" he rejoiced. "I knew she was bound to call sooner or later." He never answered a phone so fast in his whole life.

"Hey, Jerome, it's Steven," said Steven. "What are you doing tonight?"

"Oh, it's you," answered Jerome sadly. "I was just thinking of making a noose to put around my neck. Then I was going to jump off the coffee table and hang myself."

"You still haven't heard from Ginger, huh?" asked Steven.

"No, man. That woman must be made out of steel to carry a grudge this long. No sense of loyalty! Say, how's your yoga coming along? Have you found the true meaning of life yet?" Jerome kidded.

"Look, Jerome, don't joke about the yoga classes. You don't even know what you're talking about," said Steven sharply.

"I'm sorry. I really am sorry. I can't seem to say anything pleasant to anybody these days. Please forgive me," said Jerome.

"Forgiven," said Steven. "Now, what I called you to find out is if you'll come with me to a party at Holly's place tonight."

"Who's Holly?" asked Jerome.

"She's in my yoga class," Steven answered. "In fact, most of the people she's invited are in the class. She's making up a batch of health food sandwiches and brownies that she wants us to sample for this health food cookbook she's writing."

"Sure, why not," Jerome said. "It beats sitting on a stool in some bar."

"Great!" said Steven. "I'll pick you up around quarter after eight. Okay?"

"Okay. Say, Steve?"

"Yeah?" Steven answered.

"Thanks for calling."

1 **About the Story.** Answer these questions.

1. Why was Jerome thinking about going out to have a drink?

_____

2. At first, who did Jerome think was calling him on the phone?

_____

3. How did Jerome react when he found out Steven was calling?

_____

4. How did Steven react when Jerome poked fun at his yoga classes?

_____

5. Why had Steven called Jerome?

_____

6. Why does Jerome agree to go to Holly's party?

_____

7. What is the difference between how Jerome acts at the beginning of the phone call and how he acts at the end of the phone call?

_____

_____

What do you think?

8. What is one rule you think Jerome has about how to treat women?

_____

9. Is Jerome the kind of person you would like to have as a friend?
   (Be sure to explain your answer.)

_____

_____

2 The Ending -en. Use the words at the left to fill in the blanks.

broken
chosen
forgiven
forgotten
frozen
loosen
mistaken
moisten
sunken
threaten
weaken
written

1. The ground beef was so _____ that Joyce knew it would never thaw in time for dinner, so she decided to eat out that night.

2. Steven had _____ Jerome for the rude jokes he made on the phone about yoga classes.

3. After two hours of hard work, the divers were able to hoist

   the _____ chest up to the boat.

4. Mack had been so busy working on the plans for the new computer that

   he had _____ all about his wife's birthday.

5. When he woke up the next morning, the boxer wondered if winning

   the fight was really worth a _____ jaw.

6. The manager had _____ Ann to go to the sales meeting in New York.

7. The doctor told Kate that smoking a pack of cigarettes a day would

   surely _____ her heart.

8. The letter had been _____ on such thin paper that Louise ripped it badly when she unfolded it.

9. Mrs. Scott certainly didn't want to _____ her children, but she didn't know any other way to get them to do their chores around the house.

10. Butch was wheezing so badly that he decided to _____ his tie so he could breathe better.

11. Because Ruth didn't _____ the stamp enough, it came off the letter as soon as she put it in the mailbox.

12. "If you think I'm going to wash all these dishes while you sit there and watch

    television, you're sadly _____!" exclaimed Mike.

3 **Which Word Does Not Fit?** Choose the word in each line that does not fit with the rest and write it on the line to the right.

1. brother   buddy   mother   sister   grandfather   _____

2. hail   ice   ice cubes   sleet   slush   _____

3. blouse   jeans   pants   slacks   trousers   _____

4. butter   flour   salt   sugar   chocolate cake   _____

5. bake   beef   broil   fry   roast   _____

6. roar   scream   shout   speak   yell   _____

7. blackbird   crow   worm   wren   woodpecker   _____

8. bag   purse   trip   knapsack   suitcase   _____

9. heart   lung   nose   breathing   bloodstream   _____

10. chore   job   play   task   work   _____

Lesson 10

The Sound for _au_

haul	cause	auto	sauce	pause	caught
Paul	because	automobile	saucer	gauze	taught
fault	caution	autumn	saucepan	haunt	daughter
faulty	cautious	August	faucet	haunted	slaughter
				laundry	laundromat

Words for Study

search	spoke	slot	together
machines	responded	straightened	neither
completed	half	repeated	nor

Jerome Goes to the Laundromat

Jerome hauled his laundry out to his automobile and threw it in the trunk. It was a rainy autumn morning, and Jerome decided he might as well do his laundry now and get it over with.

The laundromat was always such a drag. First you had to search for a parking space. Then you had to get your clothes from the trunk of the car to the machines without dropping them all over the place. Then you had to hope the machines were working properly. The last concern, of course, was getting all the clothes back home without losing anything.

Today wasn't so bad though. The only other person there was Holly. She had just found a machine that worked after having lost four quarters and two dimes. Not only was Jerome glad to see her again, but also she could tell him which machines to avoid.

"Hey, Holly," Jerome said. "Remember me? I'm a friend of Steve's. He brought me to your party last Saturday."

"Of course, I remember you," responded Holly who had just completed writing "Out of Order" signs for two of the washing machines. "It's good to see you again. You were feeling bad about some girl that night, weren't you?"

"Yeah, her name's Ginger," answered Jerome. "I still haven't seen her."

Holly thought for a moment before she spoke. "Have you tried?"

"Nope," said Jerome as he paused to empty a half cupful of soap into the machine and push in the slot. "How about that!" he exclaimed. "On the first try, I got a machine that works right!"

"I don't understand you at all," said Holly. "If you like this girl so much, why don't you try to see her and get things straightened out?"

"Because," Jerome explained, "it's her fault."

"Even so, you're the one who wants to see her."

"It's her fault," Jerome repeated. "She's the one who hung up on me, so she's the one who should call up and say how sorry she is for being such a jerk."

"If anybody is a jerk, Jerome, it's you," said Holly.

"You women," laughed Jerome. "You stick together like glue. Well, just to show you there's no hard feelings, I'll buy you a Coke." He put quarters into the Coke machine, but neither Coke nor his quarters came out.

"Serves you right," laughed Holly.

1 **About the Story.** Answer these questions.

1. List three reasons that explain why Jerome thought going to the laundromat was a drag.

   a. _____

   b. _____

   c. _____

2. Describe what Holly was doing when Jerome came into the laundromat.

   _____

3. How many washing machines did Holly try before she found one that worked?

   _____

4. What two clues in the story told you how many washing machines Holly tried before she found one that worked?

   a. _____

   b. _____

5. Why hadn't Jerome called up Ginger yet?

   _____

6. Why did Holly think that Jerome should call up Ginger?

   _____

7. Why did Holly tell Jerome that he was a jerk?

   _____

What do you think?

8. Do you think Jerome should call up Ginger? Why or why not?

_____

_____

2 **More Work with the Ending -en.** Use the words at the left to fill in the blanks.

beaten
bitten
driven
eaten
fallen
given
ridden
risen
rotten
shaken
spoken
straightened

1. Because a new driver had _____ the bus on Monday, it was twenty minutes late.

2. Bucky decided to put off raking his yard until all the leaves had _____ from the trees.

3. Lee was so _____ when she fell off the horse that she vowed she would never ride again.

4. The dentist told Mr. Downs that it would cost over a thousand dollars to have his daughter's teeth _____.

5. What does it mean when somebody tells you that you have _____ off more than you can chew?

6. After the Brown children had _____ their Thanksgiving dinner, they were so full that they had no room for the pie.

7. Paul had not _____ to Joyce for so long that he had forgotten what her voice sounded like.

8. Even though the team was badly _____, the fans clapped loyally as the players came off the field.

9. Tim would have _____ his daughter a lift into town, but she wanted to walk with her friends.

10. Have you ever _____ in a buggy drawn by a team of horses?

11. "Christ the Lord is _____ Today" is a song that many Christians sing on Easter Sunday.

12. When you have had a _____ day at work, do you look forward to better days, or do you feel that everything is hopeless?

3 **Which Word Does Not Fit?** Choose the word in each line that does not fit with the rest and write it on the line to the right.

1. newspaper	reporter	teacher	teller	writer	_____
2. August	February	January	May	month	_____
3. ace	deck	jack	king	queen	_____
4. brick	building	iron	steel	wood	_____
5. ant	flea	gnat	honeybee	pest	_____
6. blues	drum	folk	jazz	rock and roll	_____
7. cup	glass	plate	saucer	saucepan	_____
8. auto	highway	jeep	truck	van	_____
9. chestnut	elm	ivy	oak	pine	_____
10. autumn	season	spring	summer	winter	_____
11. catfish	eel	perch	shark	whale	_____
12. England	France	Rome	Spain	Sweden	_____

4 **Spelling Check.** The answers to the clues are listed at the left. As you can see, the letters of the words are all mixed up. Spell the words the right way on the lines.

1. a a b e f k r s t _____ This is the first meal of the day.

2. a a b e h l p t _____ This begins with the letter *a* and ends with the letter *z*.

3. a a m m m l _____ This animal feeds its young with milk.

4. a C h i m r s s t _____ Some people celebrate this day by giving gifts which have been placed under a tree or in stockings.

5. c d o o r t _____ Some people go to this person when they feel sick.

6. c e e f f o _____ Some people like it black; others put cream and sugar in it.

7. e d d g i n w _____ You will find a bride and groom here.

8. i m o r r r _____ You look at yourself in this to make sure you look all right.

9. i S s s w _____ This kind of cheese has holes in it.

10. e e h i n r t t _____ Many people think this number brings bad luck.

Lesson 11

Review of the r-Controlled Vowel

ar:	darn	harp	lard	barge	charge	barber	farther	apart
er:	concert	cancer	perk	Herb	herb	berserk	weren't	nervous
ir:	sir	Kirk	chirp	birch	fir	circus	circle	squirm
or:	cord	cork	corpse	forbid	forth	forge	gorge	Norway
ur:	fur	surf	blurt	lurch	murder	murmur	hurl	jury

Words for Study

piece	daydreaming	remains
bordered	breed	spied
peanut	listen	single

The Camping Trip

Even if Jerome had decided to call Ginger, he wouldn't have been able to reach her. In the first place, Ginger had had her phone taken out. As Ginger saw it, no phone would mean one less bill to pay. In the second place, Ginger had gone to camp out on a piece of land she owned up north. This was just what she needed, she reasoned, to perk her up after her trouble with Jerome. Men!

On the third day Ginger was camping, she hiked on a path that she hadn't been on before. The path was bordered by huge fir trees and pine trees. Birds chirped from the branches, and squirrels searched for food.

After Ginger had hiked about five miles, she sat down under a birch tree and gorged on peanut butter sandwiches and brownies. How peaceful it was! There was no way that anybody could barge in on her here: no newspapers filled with the latest murder stories and cancer scares; no shows or concerts to have to get ready for.

Ginger did not have to report back to the band until next Thursday. She was daydreaming about never having to work again when she thought she heard a growling sound from farther down the path.

"Oh, no!" cried Ginger. Her pleasant daydream quickly turned into an awful picture of being eaten by some strange breed of wild animal. "Why," thought Ginger out loud, "didn't I listen to my mother?" Ginger's mother was always harping on the fact that young ladies *never* go camping alone.

By now, Ginger was so nervous that she couldn't tell if she had really heard an animal or not. However, this was certainly no time to go berserk. She calmly put the remains of her lunch in her knapsack, slowly got up, and then ran for her life. The once-peaceful woods now seemed filled with strange and threatening sounds.

Ginger had run about half a mile when she spied two fishermen wading in a stream. She yelled with all her might to the men, who were so surprised that they nearly lost their footing and fell into the stream.

"When I get back to the city," screamed Ginger as she lurched toward the men, "I'm going to buy a phone for every room, paint all the walls, and read every single newspaper I can find!"

Needless to say, the men thought she was nuts.

1 **About the Story.** Answer these questions.

1. Give two reasons why Jerome couldn't have gotten in touch with Ginger even if he had wanted to.

   a. _____

   b. _____

2. What was Ginger daydreaming about just before she thought she heard the growl of a strange animal?

   _____

3. List three things Ginger vowed to do as soon as she got back to the city.

   a. _____

   b. _____

   c. _____

4. Why does Ginger now look forward to her life in the city?

   _____

5. In one or two sentences, tell what happened in this story.

   _____

   _____

What do you think?

6. Do you think Ginger really heard a wild animal? Give a reason for your answer.

_____

7. Do you feel safer in the city or the woods?

_____

2 **Words That Begin with _re-_.** Use the words at the left to fill in the blanks.
(Use the rules you have learned to sound out the new words.)

react
recall
recover
refuse
rejected
rejection
remarks
repeat
require
respect
reveal

1. The main reason that Jerome didn't call Ginger was that he had no idea

   how she would _____.

2. He didn't want to face the fact that Ginger might _____ to see
   him again.

3. Jerome made some rude _____ about Ginger.

4. However, the truth was that he had a lot of _____ for her.

5. His problem was that he didn't want to _____ his true feelings
   to Ginger because he thought he might get hurt.

6. Jerome could still _____ the first time a girl had told him
   she didn't want to see him anymore.

7. It had happened during his second year of high school, and it had taken him

   the rest of high school to _____ from it.

8. Jerome certainly didn't want to _____ this kind of pain with Ginger.

9. None of us likes to be _____, but Jerome was so scared

   of _____ that it kept him from calling a person he really loved.

10. Jerome would _____ a lot more than just one talk in the
    laundromat with Holly to change his mind.

3 **Words That Mean the Same.** Match the words at the left with the words at the right that mean nearly the same thing.

boast   _____   1. awful

faithful

juicy   _____   2. answer

lousy   _____   3. brag

mistaken

nervous   _____   4. celebrate

recall   _____   5. edgy

rejoice

require   _____   6. loyal

respond

     _____   7. moist

     _____   8. need

     _____   9. remember

     _____   10. wrong

4 **What is Where?** Put the words at the left under the proper heading.

bleach	**A Laundromat**	**A Library**	**A Diner**
bookshelves			
coin machines	1. _____	1. _____	1. _____
dryers			
grill	2. _____	2. _____	2. _____
newspapers	3. _____	3. _____	3. _____
oven			
records			
tips			

5 **What is Where?** Put the words at the left under the proper heading.

center field	**A Circus**	**A Concert**	**A Baseball Game**
clowns			
dancing bears	1. _____	1. _____	1. _____
drums			
flutes	2. _____	2. _____	2. _____
pitchers	3. _____	3. _____	3. _____
scoreboards			
side shows			
stage			

Lesson 12

Review of Vowels Followed by the Letter /

al:	gall	mall	malt	palm	waltz	wallet	Walter	
el:	elf	elk	elbow	jelly	Jello	hotel	motel	shelter
il:	dill	sill	silk	pill	pillow	filter	wilt	William
ol:	colt	volt	mold	moldy	roller	holder		
ul:	gulp	gulf	gull	gully	sulk	sulky	bulk	bulky

Words for Study

informed	overcoat	supposed
cheer	excited	spangled
onto	ulcers	banner

The Football Game

Steven's boss had given him two free passes to Sunday's football game between the Colts and the Cowboys. Holly had agreed to go with him. He could tell that it was going to be a strange afternoon because Holly had asked if they could sit behind the batter's box.

"That's baseball," Steven informed her. "Just bring a pillow to sit on. I think it's going to be a long afternoon."

Once they found their seats, Steven took a dollar from his wallet and bought a box of buttered popcorn. After he had poured some into the palm of Holly's hand, he ate some of the popcorn himself. "A dollar for a box of moldy popcorn!" Steven exclaimed.

"Don't start sulking," said Holly. "Here come the teams." As the crowd stood up to cheer the players onto the field, the man next to Steven bumped him in the chest with his elbow. The buttered popcorn spilled all over Steven's coat and trousers.

Steven was just about to make a nasty remark to the man when Holly said, "Steven, don't be sulky. The game is starting."

"Holly," responded Steven, "it isn't time for the game yet. The teams are just warming up."

"Oh," said Holly. "Who's that man in the overcoat who keeps walking back and forth and shouting at the players?"

"That's the coach," answered Steven.

"He must have ulcers if he shouts like that all the time. What's the matter? Doesn't he like his job?" Holly asked.

"He's just getting his men excited about the game, so they play well," Steven answered.

"Why?" asked Holly.

"Holly, football isn't like yoga. Yoga is supposed to be peaceful. Football is supposed to be like a battle. Each team has an hour to score more touchdowns than the other team."

"You mean all these people drove all the way down here and paid money to see something that only lasts an hour?" asked Holly.

"Well, with flags on the plays and half time," explained Steven, "the game lasts more than sixty minutes. It's just that the playing time is only an hour."

"What's a flag on the play?" asked Holly.

Just then, the band began to play "The Star Spangled Banner." Everyone stood up and turned to face the flag. Steven guessed what Holly's next question would be and said, "No, Holly, this is not what is meant by a flag on the play. Will you please relax? The game will begin in a few minutes."

1 **About the Story.** Answer these questions.

1. Who had given Steven the free passes to the game?

_____

2. Which teams were playing that Sunday?

_____

3. Give two examples which show that Holly knows nothing about football.

   a. _____

   b. _____

4. Describe what happened to Steven's buttered popcorn.

_____

5. What song is played before the start of a football game?

_____

6. Do you think Holly knows much about baseball? Give a reason for your answer.

_____

_____

What do you think?

7. Suppose you had been sitting in front of Steven and Holly. Would you have enjoyed listening to them? Give a reason for your answer.

_____

_____

2 **More Work with Words That Begin with *re-*.** Use the words at the left to fill in the blanks. (Use the rules you have learned to sound out the new words.)

reduce
refreshed
related
remove
repair
reply
report
retired
retreat
return
revive
recovery

1. The lifeguards worked hard to _____ the swimmer who had passed out in the deep end of the pool.

2. Dick was unable to _____ the grease stains from his shirt, so he decided to use it as a rag.

3. Grace knew her mother would hit the ceiling when she saw her _____ card.

4. Luke didn't get the grass cut last Saturday because it took him all afternoon to _____ the lawn mower.

5. After a long, hot shower, William felt so _____ that the last thing he felt like doing was his homework.

6. Kirk had put on twenty-three pounds during the winter months, and he knew he would have to _____ if his spring clothes were going to fit him properly.

7. The first thing Louise wanted to do when she _____ from her job was move to a warmer state.

8. Walter was surprised when his mother told him that all the people who had come to the wedding were _____ to him.

9. After Rose's _____, the doctor told her that she still had to take it easy for a few months.

10. On her way to the movie, Mrs. Hall stopped by the library to _____ the two books she had taken out last month.

11. After the battle, the army was ordered to _____ to a hill further away from the field.

12. Ruth hoped she would get a quick _____ to her letter because she needed a job very badly.

3 **Word Opposites.** Match the words at the left with the words that are opposite in meaning.

fallen
forgive
listen
moldy
nervous
scratchy
sunless
reveal
wasteful
wilt

_____ 1. blame

_____ 2. bloom

_____ 3. calm

_____ 4. fresh

_____ 5. hide

_____ 6. risen

_____ 7. smooth

_____ 8. speak

_____ 9. sunny

_____ 10. thrifty

4 **Compound Words.** To find the answers, choose a word from **List A** and add a word from **List B** to it. Study the example before you begin.

List A	List B
black	back
court	basket
day	break
dead	ground
egg	line
✓ foot	✓ print
home	room
luke	shell
play	sick
quarter	still
stand	top
waste	warm

footprint   1. This word is a mark made by the foot in dirt or sand.

_____ 2. In a football game, he throws passes or runs with the ball.

_____ 3. This word is the hard covering of a bird's egg.

_____ 4. This word is the latest time by which something must be done.

_____ 5. This word describes a longing to be home.

_____ 6. This is another word for dawn.

_____ 7. This is another word for everything coming to a complete stop.

_____ 8. This is for papers and other trash that you want to throw away.

_____ 9. This is used to pave roads and highways.

_____ 10. This is where the jury sits to hear a case.

_____ 11. This word describes something that is neither hot nor cold.

_____ 12. You find children playing on swings and slides here.

Word Index: Lessons 1-12

A
actor
ad
advice
afford
afterward
agree
ahoy
aim
already
although
anymore
apart
apartment
ape
armful
August
auto
automobile
autumn
avoid

B
backfire
bait
banner
barber
barge
basketball
bathing
bead
beast
beaten
bedding
beginning
bench
berserk
besides
billfold
bin
birch
bitch
bitten
blackboard
blacktop
blade
blank
blast
blend
blessing
blindly
bloody
bloom
blues
blurt
boast
bobsled
boiler

bookcase
bookshelf
bookworm
boom
booty
bop
border
bossy
bound
Boy Scout
brace
bracelet
brag
braid
brainy
branch
breast
breathing
breed
breeze
bribe
broil
broken
brook
brought
brownie
bruise
brush
buggy
building
bulk
bulky
Butch
buzz

C
camping
cancer
carpenter
caution
cautious
certainly
chalk
chalkboard
charge
cheapskate
cheat
cheer
chirp
chore
chose
chosen
chow
chunk
circle
circus
clam
clash

classroom
clearing
clench
clerk
cliff
clipping
clothing
clung
clutter
coffeecake
colt
comeback
coming
complain
complete
concern
concert
confuse
cord
cork
cornstarch
corpse
cost
costly
counter
countless
courtroom
cove
covering
cramp
crate
crew
crosswalk
crow
crude
cruise
cruiser
crutch
crybaby
cud
cuff
cutting

D
daily
darn
daughter
daybreak
daydream
deadline
dense
dentist
difference
dill
dirty
dishpan
dishrag
doggy

dome
doorknob
dose
drape
drawn
dread
dreadful
dreamer
dreamland
drench
dressing
drift
drill
drip
driven
drug
drugstore
dryer
dummy

E
earring
eaten
edgy
egghead
elbow
elf
elk
enjoy
enter
etc.
eve
excite
exclaim
exercise
expect
eyesight
eyestrain

F
faith
faithful
fallen
family
farther
fate
faucet
fault
faulty
feast
feather
filter
finger
fingernail
fingerprint
fir
firelight
fisherman

fitting
flap
flashlight
flea
fleet
flight
flip
flirt
flowerpot
flute
folk(s)
footing
footprint
forbid
force
forge
forgive
forgiven
forgotten
forth
freeway
freshly
freshman
fright
frighten
frog
frozen
fruit
fruitcake
fur

G
Gail
gale
gall
gauze
gaze
geese
given
glance
globe
gloom
gloomy
glove
glow
gnarled
gnash
gnat
gnaw
gnawing
gnome
goof
gorge
gosh
grace
grain
grandfather
grandmother

grapefruit
grease
Greece
greedy
Greek
greet
grill
grind
grouchy
growl
grownup
grudge
gulf
gull
gully
gulp
gumdrop

H
hairy
half
handshake
happiness
hardware
harp
Harvey
haul
haunt
haunted
health
healthy
hem
herb
Herb
highness
highway
hiss
hoist
holder
Holly
homemade
homesick
homey
hotel
hourly
housewife
how's
huh
hurl

I
icing
improve
inform
inside
invite
involve
ivy

J
Jello
jelly
Jerome
jet
Joyce
joyful
judge
juice
juicy
jumpy
jury

K
kin
kinfolk(s)
Kirk
kitchen
knack
knapsack
kneecap
knelt
knickknack
knight
knob
knockout
knot
knotty

L
lard
lately
laundromat
laundry
lawyer
leaky
leap
leapfrog
leash
leather
ledge
Lee
lesson
library
lifeguard
lighten
lighthouse
lining
listen
lively
lodge
longing
loose
loosen
lousy
lower
loyally
loyalty

Luke
lukewarm
lurch

M
machine
madly
mailbox
mailman
mall
malt
mankind
Mansfield
Martin
mash
matchbook
Matthew
meatball
mighty
mildly
mist
mistaken
moan
moist
moisten
mold
moldy
moment
moose
mope
motel
murder
murmur

N
nasty
nearby
neatly
neither
nervous
newspaper
newsstand
nonsense
nook
noose
nor
Norway
notch
notice
nudge

O
oak
oat
oatmeal
oddly
oh
onto
ooze

overboard
overcoat
overgrown
overhead
owe
ox

P

pact
padding
painful
painless
palm
paste
patty
Paul
pause
pave
paving
peaceful
peacefully
peanut
peeler
perch
perk
phony
piece
pigpen
pill
pillow
pinch
pitch
pitcher
pitchfork
plainly
playground
plea
plead
pleasant
pleased
pledge
plenty
plow
plump
poach
porch
pounce
pout
practice
praise
press

pretty
prince
probably
prop
proper
properly
pry
puffy
putty

Q

quarter
quarterback

R

raft
rag
railroad
rainy
rarely
rash
recall
recover
recovery
reduce
reform
refresh
reject
rejection
rejoice
remains
remark
repair
repeat
reply
reporter
require
respect
respond
restless
restroom
retire
retreat
reveal
revive
ridden
ridge
ringside
rinse
risen
risky
roadwork

roller
roof
rosebud
rotten
route
royally
royalty
runny
rut
Ruth

S

sailor
salty
Sam
sample
sandwich
sauce
saucepan
saucer
savings
scale
scald
scarecrow
scold
scoop
scorch
scoreboard
Scotch
Scott
scour
scram
scraper
scratchy
screw
script
scrounge
scruff
search
season
sex
shade
shady
shaken
shaky
shark
she'd
shelf
shelter
she's
shipwreck

shook
shopping
shortcake
shorts
shove
shyly
side show
sidewalk
sift
sigh
silk
sill
single
sir
skater
sketch
ski
skid
skillful
skinny
skip
skull
slaughter
sled
sleet
slept
slid
slide
slight
slot
slouch
slump
smack
smear
Smith
smog
smoky
smooth
smoothly
smudge
snapshot
snarl
snatch
sneak
sneakers
sneaky
sniff
snowball
snowstorm
socks

softly
spaghetti
span
spangle
spark
speck
sped
speech
spendthrift
spin
spine
splurge
spoke
spoken
spoonful
spotless
spout
sprout
spy
squarely
squeaky
squirm
stage fright
stall
standstill
starch
stash
stem
Steve
Steven
stir
stitch
stocking
stone
stony
stool
stoop
straighten
strain
strap
stray
streak
stress
stressful
strict
stuffing
stuffy
stunt
successfully
sue

sugar
sugarless
suit
suitcase
sulk
sulky
sunglasses
sunken
sunless
suppose
surf
swam
Swede
Sweden
sweep
sweeper
swept
swing
Swiss

T

tailspin
tasteless
tasty
taught
Ted
tee
teepee
teller
tense
Thanksgiving
theft
they're
thickly
thief
thinner
thirst
thirsty
thorn
thread
threat
threaten
thrift
thrifty
throat
throb
throughout
thud
thump
thus
tighten

tightly
tilt
together
toil
Tony
toolbox
toothbrush
toothpaste
trace
trainer
trance
trashy
tread
trend
tribe
tricky
troop
trooper
trounce
trousers
trout
truce
trudge
truthfully

U

ulcer
underground
undershirt
understand
unhealthy

V

van
vane
veal
vine
visit
void
volt
vow

W

waist
waistline
waiter
wallet
Walter
waltz
wander
washcloth
washing

wastebasket
watchful
watchman
weaken
weather
wedding
we'll
weren't
whack
wham
wheeze
whether
whichever
whiff
whim
whine
who's
wildly
William
wilt
window
wiring
wise
wisely
woodpecker
woodwork
woody
woolly
workshop
worthless
wrapper
wrapping
wrecker
wren
wrench
wring
wrung

X

Y

yeah
Y.M.C.A.
yoga
yogurt
you'll
you've
yuk!

Z

Lesson 13

Review of the Hard and Soft c and g

The hard c as in *candy, cost,* and *cutting:*

cannot	carpet	cardboard	cocoa	coconut
cob	cobweb	cock	cocky	cockroach

The soft c as in *cellar, city,* and *pounce:*

cider	cinder	Cinderella	cinch	
lance	prance	mince	mincemeat	dunce

The hard g as in *gas, get, goof* and *log:*

gain	gear	gob	gobble	goofy	goo
gag	tag	bingo	golly	gust	gut	gutter

The soft g as in *Ginger, George,* and *forge:*

gee	gem	gent	gentle	gentleman	gently
merge	verge	binge	singe	lunge	plunge

Words for Study

scheme	keg	afraid
halt	potato chips	except
pane	pickles	sadness

Jerome's Scheme

Jerome decided to have a party. Tony had told him that Ginger was back in town. Jerome's scheme was that Tony would invite Ginger to the party, and Ginger would agree to come. Then he and Ginger would put a halt to their fighting and get things straightened out between them. Tony agreed to this scheme, and Jerome plunged into the work of getting his apartment ready for the party.

He bought two cans of bug spray at the hardware store to get rid of the cockroaches in the kitchen. He swept the cobwebs from the top of the bookshelves and the ceiling. He cleaned the carpet and was on the verge of washing the windows when he decided, "Enough is enough! I'll just put a fresh piece of cardboard where the pane is cracked a little, and that's it. Everything looks great!"

Jerome then went on a shopping binge. He bought a quarter keg of beer, some cider, roast beef, ham, and Swiss cheese, rolls, potato chips, dill pickles, three mincemeat pies, and a huge coconut cake. As much as Jerome had enjoyed himself at Holly's party, he thought the health food was dreadful. This was going to be a real party with real food!

Jerome's party didn't really get into gear until about ten o'clock. It was the same old story: everyone was afraid to be the first guest to show up. Jerome acted as if he were very excited to see everybody, but he was waiting for only one person.

At one o'clock, Jerome's apartment was a wreck. The food had been gobbled up as if none of his friends had eaten all week. The carpet was spotted with crumbs and cigarette ashes. Paper cups and plates were everywhere. Someone had put on a slow record, and everybody was dancing—everybody, that is, except Jerome.

Jerome sat by himself in a corner of the living room. He was thinking of all the ways he could murder Tony. He had called Tony's place twice, but no one had answered. Where were those two?

Anne Clark came over and asked Jerome if he wanted to dance, but he just waved her away. He wished he could wave everybody away. How could all these people in his living room be having a good time? Were they so dumb that they couldn't see the great sadness of life? Jerome went into his bedroom and threw himself onto the bed as his friends laughed and danced until four o'clock in the morning.

1 **About the Story.** Answer these questions.

1. Why had Jerome decided to have a party?

   _____

2. How was Tony involved in Jerome's scheme?

   _____

3. List three things that Jerome did to get ready for the party.

   a. _____

   b. _____

   c. _____

4. At what time did Jerome's party really start? _____

5. At what time did Jerome's party end? _____

6. Why did Jerome have such a lousy time at his own party?

   _____

What do you think?

7. What do you think might have happened to Tony and Ginger?

   _____

2 **Words That Begin with *in-*.** Use the words at the left to fill in the blanks. Use the rules you have learned to sound out the words.

invite
invade
inhale
invent
infect
inquire
inspire
instruct
increase
intend

_____   1. to draw air into the lungs

_____   2. to make a machine or anything else that is brand-new

_____   3. to take over another person's land by force

_____   4. to ask someone to go out with you or come to your home

_____   5. to get larger in size

_____   6. to teach someone how to do something

_____   7. to ask a question

_____   8. to cause to become sick

_____   9. to have something in mind; to plan

_____   10. to fill someone with hope

3 **Which Word Fits Best?** Choose the right word from the four choices and put it on the line.

1. Bark is to dog as _____ is to bird.
   (a) branch   (b) chirp   (c) nest   (d) wing

2. Belt is to waist as scarf is to _____ .
   (a) cloth   (b) coat   (c) neck   (d) wrap

3. State is to California as city is to _____ .
   (a) Boston   (b) country   (c) sidewalks   (d) subway

4. Dill pickle is to sour as _____ is to sweet.
   (a) coffeecake   (b) grapefruit   (c) spaghetti   (d) plain yogurt

5. Reveal is to hide as respect is to _____ .
   (a) hidden   (b) look down upon   (c) look up to   (d) love

6. Gill is to fish as _____ is to human being.
   (a) air   (b) breath   (c) breathe   (d) lung

7. Wade is to water as hike is to _____ .
   (a) boots   (b) land   (c) march   (d) trudge

8. Ice is to solid as _____ is to gas.
   (a) liquid   (b) steam   (c) stove   (d) water

9. Overdone is to raw as _____ is to fresh.
   (a) new   (b) ripe   (c) rude   (d) stale

10. Then is to now as past is to _____ .
    (a) last year   (b) next year   (c) present   (d) tomorrow

11. Murmur is to soft as _____ is to loud.
    (a) inform   (b) instruct   (c) roar   (d) say

12. Sunday is to week as January is to _____ .
    (a) month   (b) thirty-one days   (c) time   (d) year

4 **Consonants.** A *consonant* is any letter of the alphabet that is not a vowel. Each of the words listed below has a double consonant. To help you sound out the word, draw a line between the double consonant and mark the *first* vowel short. Then say the word out loud. Study the example before you begin.

1. gutter   *gŭt – ter*

2. matter   _____

3. summer   _____

4. happen   _____

5. mugger   _____

6. cutting   _____

7. mammal   _____

8. catty   _____

9. pepper   _____

10. slipper   _____

Lesson 14

The *gh* and *ght* Words

fight	eight	caught	bought
sight	eighty	taught	brought
height	freight	daughter	fought
fright	weight	slaughter	sought
frighten		naughty	ought
bright			
brightly			

sigh	weigh	laugh	tough	cough	dough
high	sleigh	laughter	rough		doughnut
	neighbor		enough		
	neighborhood				

Words for Study

shown	salesman	struggle
headquarters	insisted	stutter
sake	property	sons

Whatever Happened to Tony and Ginger?

The reason Tony and Ginger hadn't shown up for Jerome's party was that they had spent most of the night at police headquarters. This is what happened.

About a year ago, Tony had bought a small house on the north side of town. For the first six months, he and his neighbor, Mrs. Darkpill, had been on very good terms. This was odd because everybody else in the neighborhood avoided Mrs. Darkpill and her three children as much as they could.

It seemed that even Mr. Darkpill avoided her. Five days a week he lived in a motel. He came home on the weekends only for the children's sake. All this time, the Darkpill children thought their father was an important salesman who was on the road most of the time. Mr. Darkpill and his wife never fought in front of the children, so they had no idea what was really going on. It did seem strange to them, however, that their mother and father rarely spoke to each other.

About four months ago, Mrs. Darkpill had begun to complain to Tony about the chestnut tree in his back yard. The tree, she insisted, was really on her property, and she wanted it cut down at once. Tony checked his deed to the property, and it was clear from the deed that Mrs. Darkpill was dead wrong.

Then Tony began to understand why the other neighbors avoided Mrs. Darkpill. Every morning at five o'clock for three weeks straight, Tony woke up to the sound of a buzz saw. It seemed that Mrs. Darkpill intended to remove all the branches of his lovely chestnut tree one by one. Tony tried to talk some sense into Mrs. Darkpill, but it didn't work.

Then one day when Tony was yelling at the Darkpill kids for climbing all over his car, Mrs. Darkpill called the police and told them that Tony had whipped her daughter just because she had touched his car. The cops knew that Mrs. Darkpill was crazy, but they couldn't do much if she decided to press charges. And that's just what Mrs. Darkpill did.

Now what does all this have to do with the fact that Tony and Ginger spent Friday night at police headquarters while Jerome was feeling so gloomy at his party? The answer to this question is in the next story.

1 **About the Story.** Answer these questions.

1. Describe how Mr. Darkpill got along with his wife.

_____

_____

2. How did the trouble between Tony and Mrs. Darkpill begin?

_____

_____

3. What did Mrs. Darkpill tell the police about Tony?

_____

4. Does Mrs. Darkpill's name seem to fit her? Why or why not?

_____

_____

What do you think?

5. What would you do if a person like Mrs. Darkpill were your neighbor?

_____

_____

2 **The *gh* and *ght* Words.** Use the words at the left to fill in each blank.

bright
cough
daughters
dough
eight
enough
height
might
neighbor
ought
right
right
rough
sighed
sleigh
tough

1. Although I do struggle with all my _____,

   I can't seem to get those *g-h-t* words _____.

2. When I see *g-h-t* words, I stutter and cough.

   Their crazy spellings just turn me _____ off.

3. I asked my _____ if he could tell why

   These rules were made, but he only _____.

4. "It's strange," he laughed sadly, "they _____ to know better

   Than to teach sons and _____ these nasty old letters."

5. Now bread's made from _____ which is smooth and not _____.

   A _____ means you're sick. Strong arms mean you're _____.

6. You ride in a _____. For basketball, you need _____.

   After seven comes _____. When the sun's out, it's _____.

7. Well, I have no idea how I'll learn all this stuff.

   I'm going out with my friends now, 'cause I've had _____!

3 **Same or Opposite?** If the words in each pair mean the same thing, write *same* on the line to the right. If they do not mean the same thing, write *opposite* on the line.

1. cocky   shy   _____

2. dense   thick   _____

3. deserve   earn   _____

4. dunce   egghead   _____

5. gain   lose   _____

6. gentle   tough   _____

7. goofy   nutty   _____

8. guide   lead   _____

9. instruct   learn   _____

10. inquire   ask   _____

11. scheme   plot   _____

12. thaw   freeze   _____

4 **More Work with Double Consonants.** Draw a line between the double consonants and mark the first vowel short. Then say the word out loud. Study the example before you begin.

1. stutter   ___stŭt - ter___

2. clutter   _____

3. bitten   _____

4. wrapper   _____

5. thinner   _____

6. hitter   _____

7. lobby   _____

8. shatter   _____

9. trapper   _____

10. common   _____

Lesson 15

Review of *r*-Controlled Vowel Combinations

air:	haircut	stairway	fairy	fairly	fairness
ear:	rear	spear	fear	beard	unclear	yearly
eer:	jeer	sheer	cheerful	cheery	Cheerios	cheerleader
oar:	soar	uproar	boardwalk	cupboard	keyboard
oor:	doorbell	doorman	doormat	poorly	poorhouse
our:	ours	ourselves	hourglass	sourball	sourpuss

Words for Study

fancy	tramp	fireplace	freak
driveway	grabbed	believe	shore
booze	piano	proudly	unit

Mrs. Darkpill

At eight o'clock that Friday evening, Ginger had stopped by to pick up Tony. Tony hadn't told her where they were going. Ginger guessed they would probably go to a movie. They decided to have a cup of coffee and listen to Tony's new tape before going out into the cold, rainy night. Tony was telling Ginger about how he had to go to court on Wednesday because of his crazy neighbor when the doorbell rang.

Tony had barely gotten to the door when in barged Mrs. Darkpill. She didn't waste any time in getting to the point. "If you're going to have girls in until all hours of the night," she roared, "at least you could make sure they don't park their fancy automobiles in front of *my* driveway."

Ginger started to say she was sorry, but Tony cut her off. "Look, Mrs. Darkpill, I'll move Ginger's car from your driveway right away. Now please take your muddy feet off my brand-new carpet and get out of here."

"How dare you talk to me like that!" screamed Mrs. Darkpill at the top of her lungs.

"Did you really come over here because of the car, or are you just looking for somebody to fight with?" asked Tony calmly.

"You watch your mouth, young man! You have no right to talk to me that way with all your women and booze and carrying on!"

Now Ginger thought Mrs. Darkpill was much more exciting than any movie she might be going to see that night, so she decided to have a little fun. "Tony only buys the best, Mrs. Darkpill. Can I get you a cup?" she asked in her friendliest voice.

Tony started to warn Ginger to stay out of this, but it was too late. Mrs. Darkpill whirled around to face Ginger. "Why, you little tramp!" she shouted. "Do you think I'm going to let you make fun of me like that?" As if she were answering her own question, she grabbed the cup from Ginger's hand and hurled it at the piano where it smashed into bits on the keyboard.

It was hard to say who was more frightened—Tony or Ginger. Ginger was the first to react. "Now look, Mrs. Darkpill, why don't we all just sit down and talk this whole thing over." Trying to calm her fear of this strange woman, Ginger put her arm around Mrs. Darkpill and started to lead her over to the couch.

"You—you—you get your hands off me," stuttered Mrs. Darkpill as she broke loose and pushed Ginger into the cupboard next to the fireplace. Every single cup, saucer, plate, and serving dish in the cupboard shattered on the floor.

"I don't believe this is happening," moaned Tony. "I haven't even made the last payment on all this stuff yet." Just then he heard a police car roar into the driveway. He guessed that the neighbors had heard the uproar and called the cops.

And that is how Ginger and Tony—and Mrs. Darkpill— happened to spend Friday night at police headquarters.

1 **About the Story.** Answer these questions.

1. What is the reason Mrs. Darkpill gives for being angry at Tony this time?

_____

2. What does Mrs. Darkpill say that causes Tony to think she is just looking for a fight?

_____

3. What are Tony and Ginger drinking? _____

4. What does Mrs. Darkpill think they are drinking? _____

5. What does Ginger say or do that causes all of Tony's dishes to break?

_____

6. Why do Ginger and Tony spend the evening at police headquarters?

_____

What do you think?

7. Do you think that an evening like the one described in the story is more exciting than going to a movie?

_____

8. What do you think is Mrs. Darkpill's problem?

_____

2 **The *ea* and *ear* Words.** Say the words in each group at the left out loud. Then fill in the blanks with the right answers.

beard
feared
head
heart

1. When Ted decided to grow a _____,

His mother's _____ beat loudly.

The neighbors will all laugh, she _____.

"How can I hold my _____ up proudly?"

freak
nearby
pleaded
repeated

2. She _____ her fears out loud to Sam,

A friend who lived _____.

She _____ with Sam to talk to Ted.

"He will be a _____!" she cried.

dread
feather
leather
mincemeat

3. Now, although Sam seemed tough as _____,

His heart was filled with _____.

For he could be knocked over with a _____;

He could be turned into _____ by Ted.

beach
cheap
headed
mean

4. For Ted was _____ and had no heart.

His friends all called him _____.

But, Sam _____ for the nearby park

And found Ted on the _____.

beard
dreadful
heard
preach

5. "I _____ you're going to grow a _____.

"Your mom thinks that it's _____."

"Don't _____ to me, old man," Ted jeered,

"Or I'll make your life more stressful."

beat
leap
sea

6. Then Ted _____ it to the diving board.

The tide was out; the _____, not deep.

Three lifeguards dragged poor Ted to shore.

It's wise to look before you _____!

3 **Syllables.** A *syllable* is a word or part of a word said as a unit. For example, *shore* has one syllable; *driveway* has two syllables; and *piano* has three syllables. Each of the words listed below has two syllables. Write these syllables on the line to the right of each word. Be sure to study the examples before you begin.

1. cardboard   *card-board*

2. brightly   *bright-ly*

3. cheerful   _____

4. subway   _____

5. proudly   _____

6. inhale   _____

7. unclear   _____

8. stairway   _____

9. cobweb   _____

10. fairness   _____

11. sadness   _____

12. invade   _____

4 **More Work with Units.** Use the words at the left to fill in the blanks. Study the example before you begin.

feet
hours
letters
✓ months
ounces
quarts
rooms
seconds
states

1. The units of a year are called _months_.

2. The units of a day are called _____.

3. The units of a minute are called _____.

4. The units of a gallon are called _____.

5. The units of a pound are called _____.

6. The units of a yard are called _____.

7. The units of the alphabet are called _____.

8. The units of a house are called _____.

9. The units of the United States are called _____.

Lesson 16

Common Word Beginnings: Part 1

de-	ex-	mis-	com-	con-
describe	explain	mistake	complain	concern
decide	expect	mistaken	complaint	confront
deserve	excite	misplace	compose	contain
defend	explode	mistreat	combine	container
depend	except	misspell	compete	control
debate	exact	mistrust	complete	consume
destroy	exactly	miscount	completely	consumer
Detroit	excuse	misjudge	commit	consent

Words for Study

commented	wisecracks	ahead
vanilla	lemon	lazy
bowl	recipe	behave

Testing Recipes

Steven sat at the table in Holly's kitchen munching on peanut butter balls. "Not bad," he commented to Holly, who was trying to store the peanut butter balls in a container faster than Steven was eating them. "What's in them?"

"Rolled oats, milk, peanut butter, honey, salt, vanilla, and chopped nuts," answered Holly. "Enough of the peanut butter balls. Now try some of this." She pushed a bowl in front of Steven.

"What is it?" asked Steven. "It looks exactly like baby food—after the baby has spit it out."

"Why don't you decide what it's like after you taste it?" laughed Holly. "I'm never going to get this cookbook ready with food experts like you making wisecracks all the time."

"Yuk! Holly, this is awful. It's prunes. I hate prunes!"

"Prune whip to be exact," said Holly. "Prunes combined with lemon juice, honey, and egg whites. Very good for what ails you."

"Nothing is ailing me except this awful taste in my mouth," replied Steven. "If I were you, I'd destroy this recipe at once. Let me test the peanut butter balls again."

"Is the prune whip really that bad?"

"Here," said Steven, "go ahead and try some. Be my guest."

"Well," said Holly after trying a spoonful, "I'm not going to debate with you on this one," and she tore up the recipe card. As she checked the two pans of date-nut bread in the oven, she asked, "How's Jerome doing? Does he still think the world's giving him a raw deal?"

"He's a little better," responded Steven. "What's crazy is that he found out why Ginger never made it to the party, and he still won't call her."

"As far as I'm concerned," said Holly, "Jerome is one of those men who will never commit himself to doing the things you have to do in order to get what you want in life. Then he spends all his time complaining about how other people let you down or are lazy or dumb."

"You're being a bit hard on him, aren't you?" asked Steven. "He's not down on other people. It's just that he has these silly rules about how people should behave, and he can't see that the rules might have been good at one time, but they're kind of useless now. Jerome's a very complex person, Holly. It's not really fair of you to judge him like that."

"I'm not judging him," exclaimed Holly. "I'm just telling you what I see."

"Well," grinned Steven, "let me tell you what I see. I see smoke coming out of the oven."

"Oh, no!" groaned Holly. "The date-nut bread! I completely forgot about it!"

---

1 **About the Story.** Answer these questions.

1. List three recipes that Holly was testing.

   a. _____

   b. _____

   c. _____

2. Why was Holly testing these recipes?

   _____

3. Which recipe did Steven think was good? _____

4. Which recipe did Steven think was awful? _____

5. What did Holly think Jerome's problem was?

_____

6. What did Steven think Jerome's problem was?

_____

7. What happened to the third recipe that Holly was testing?

_____

What do you think?

8. Who do you think is right about Jerome—Holly or Steven? Be sure to explain your answer.

_____

_____

9. Which of Holly's recipes would you enjoy the most?

_____

2 **Sounds for *ow*.** Fill in the blanks with the words at the left.

bowl
bowling
cow
crowbar
elbow
flowerpot
grownups
pillow
rowboat
scarecrows
shower
towel rack

_____ 1. This word is a container for plants.

_____ 2. This is a game in which you try for strikes and spares.

_____ 3. This is a dish for serving oatmeal or prune whip.

_____ 4. This is a straight bar of iron or steel that is used to move or lift something.

_____ 5. Farmers put these in their fields to help keep their crops safe from the crows.

_____ 6. Many people put their heads on this when they go to sleep.

_____ 7. This is the joint or bend of the arm.

_____ 8. The pitcher goes here after he's been sent out of the baseball game.

_____ 9. This is what most children call older people.

_____ 10. You find this in the bathroom next to the wash basin.

_____ 11. You need a pair of oars to get across a lake in this.

_____ 12. You'll find this animal in a herd in a field or on the range.

3 **More Work with Syllables.** In the box below are some syllables that you can use to make words. The words will fit the eight sentences. No syllable is used twice, and no syllables should be left over when you are done. The number after the sentence tells you how many syllables are in each word. Study the example before you begin.

ci	Cin	cop	d~~a~~y	der	dro	el	er	hang	hel
i	la	laun	mat	o	pe	peck	re	t~~e~~r	ter
thrift	ver	wood	y	y~~e~~s					

yesterday   1. This is what the day before today is called. (3)

_____ 2. This is one kind of bird. (3)

_____ 3. This is the name of a girl in a fairy tale who lost her slipper at the prince's ball. (4)

_____ 4. This machine flies in the sky and can land on the top of buildings. (4)

_____ 5. If you don't own a washing machine, this is where you go to do your washing. (3)

_____ 6. This instructs a cook in how to make a certain food. (3)

_____ 7. If you have too much booze to drink, this is what you have when you wake up. (3)

_____ 8. This word describes a person who is careful with his money. (2)

4 **Brain Benders.** Do you know what the experts tell us about food? Answer *true* or *false* to these ten sentences. (If you don't know the answer, make a good guess.)

_____ 1. Coffee and doughnuts are a good breakfast.

_____ 2. Coffee and tea are both drugs.

_____ 3. Dinner is the most important meal of the day.

_____ 4. Eating chocolate is a quick way to pep yourself up, but the feeling does not last very long.

_____ 5. Fresh fruit juice is better for you than canned fruit juice.

_____ 6. In most cases, people who eat healthy foods feel far less stress in their lives than people who eat anything they feel like having.

_____ 7. In most cases, raw foods are better for you than cooked foods.

_____ 8. Meat, chicken, and fish are best for your health if they have been fried.

_____ 9. Sugar is not at all harmful.

_____ 10. The food you eat has nothing to do with how you feel.

Word Index: Lessons 1-16

A
actor
ad
advice
afford
afraid
afterward
agree
ahead
ahoy
aim
already
although
anymore
apart
apartment
ape
armful
August
auto
automobile
autumn
avoid

B
backfire
bait
banner
barber
barge
basketball
bathing
bead
beard
beast
beaten
bedding
beginning
behave
believe
bench
bender
berserk
besides
billfold
bin
binge
bingo
birch
bitch
bitten
blackboard
blacktop
blade
blank
blast
blend

blessing
blindly
bloody
bloom
blues
blurt
boardwalk
boast
bobsled
boiler
bookcase
bookshelf
bookworm
boom
booty
booze
bop
border
bossy
bound
bowl
bowling
Boy Scout
brace
bracelet
brag
braid
brainy
branch
breast
breathing
breed
breeze
bribe
brightly
broil
broken
brook
brought
brownie
bruise
brush
buggy
building
bulk
bulky
Butch
buzz

C
camping
cancer
cannot
cardboard
carpenter
carpet
caution

cautious
certainly
chalk
chalkboard
charge
cheapskate
cheat
cheer
cheerful
Cheerios
cheerleader
cheery
chip
chirp
chore
chose
chosen
chow
chunk
cider
cinch
cinder
Cinderella
circle
circus
clam
clash
classroom
clearing
clench
clerk
cliff
clipping
clothing
clung
clutter
cob
cobweb
cock
cockroach
cocky
cocoa
coconut
coffeecake
colt
combine
comeback
coming
comment
commit
compete
complain
complaint
complete
completely
compose

concern
concert
confront
confuse
consent
consonant
consume
consumer
contain
container
control
cord
cork
cornstarch
corpse
cost
costly
cough
counter
countless
courtroom
cove
covering
cramp
crate
crew
crosswalk
crow
crowbar
crude
cruise
cruiser
crutch
crybaby
cud
cuff
cupboard
cutting

D
daily
darn
daughter
daybreak
daydream
deadline
debate
defend
dense
dentist
depend
destroy
Detroit
difference
dill
dirty
dishpan

dishrag
doggy
dome
doorbell
doorknob
doorman
doormat
dose
dough
doughnut
drape
drawn
dread
dreadful
dreamer
dreamland
drench
dressing
drift
drill
drip
driven
driveway
drug
drugstore
dryer
dummy
dunce

E
earring
eaten
edgy
egghead
elbow
elf
elk
enjoy
enter
etc.
eve
exact
exactly
except
excite
exclaim
excuse
exercise
expect
explode
eyesight
eyestrain

F
fairly
fairness
fairy
faith

faithful
fallen
family
fancy
farther
fate
faucet
fault
faulty
fear
feast
feather
filter
finger
fingernail
fingerprint
fir
firelight
fireplace
fisherman
fitting
flap
flashlight
flea
fleet
flight
flip
flirt
flowerpot
flute
folk(s)
footing
footprint
forbid
force
forge
forgive
forgiven
forgotten
forth
freak
freeway
freight
freshly
freshman
fright
frighten
frog
frozen
fruit
fruitcake
fur

G
gag
Gail
gain

gale
gall
gauze
gaze
gear
gee
geese
gem
gent
gentle
gentleman
gently
given
glance
globe
gloom
gloomy
glove
glow
gnarled
gnash
gnat
gnaw
gnawing
gnome
gob
gobble
golly
goo
goof
goofy
gorge
gosh
grab
grace
grain
grandfather
grandmother
grapefruit
grease
Greece
greedy
Greek
greet
grill
grind
grouchy
growl
grownup
grudge
gulf
gull
gully
gulp
gumdrop
gust

gut
gutter

H
haircut
hairy
half
halt
handshake
happiness
hardware
harp
Harvey
haul
haunt
haunted
headquarters
health
healthy
height
hem
herb
Herb
highness
highway
hiss
hoist
holder
Holly
homemade
homesick
homey
hotel
hourglass
hourly
housewife
how's
huh
hurl

I
icing
improve
increase
infect
inform
inhale
inquire
inside
insist
inspire
instruct
intend
invade
invent
invite
involve
ivy

J
jeer
Jello

jelly
Jerome
jet
Joyce
joyful
judge
juice
juicy
jumpy
jury

K
keg
keyboard
kin
kinfolk(s)
Kirk
kitchen
knack
knapsack
kneecap
knelt
knickknack
knight
knob
knockout
knot
knotty

L
lance
lard
lately
laughter
laundromat
laundry
lawyer
lazy
leaky
leap
leapfrog
leash
leather
ledge
Lee
lemon
lesson
library
lifeguard
lighten
lighthouse
lining
listen
lively
lodge
longing
loose
loosen
lousy
lower
loyally

loyalty
Luke
lukewarm
lunge
lurch

M
machine
madly
mailbox
mailman
mall
malt
mankind
Mansfield
Martin
mash
matchbook
Matthew
meatball
merge
mighty
mildly
mince
mincemeat
miscount
misjudge
misplace
misspell
mist
mistaken
mistreat
mistrust
moan
moist
moisten
mold
moldy
moment
moose
mope
motel
murder
murmur

N
nasty
naughty
nearby
neatly
neighbor
neighborhood
neither
nervous
newspaper
newsstand
nonsense
nook
noose
nor
Norway

notch
notice
nudge

O
oak
oat
oatmeal
oddly
oh
onto
ooze
ought
ours
ourselves
overboard
overcoat
overgrown
overhead
owe
ox

P
pact
padding
painful
painless
palm
pane
paste
patty
Paul
pause
pave
paving
peaceful
peacefully
peanut
peeler
perch
perk
phony
piano
pickle
piece
pigpen
pill
pillow
pinch
pitch
pitcher
pitchfork
plainly
playground
plea
plead
pleasant
pleased
pledge
plenty
plow
plump

plunge
poach
poorhouse
poorly
porch
potato
potato chip
pounce
pout
practice
praise
prance
press
pretty
prince
probably
prop
proper
properly
property
proudly
pry
puffy
putty

Q
quarter
quarterback

R
raft
rag
railroad
rainy
rarely
rash
rear
recall
recipe
recover
recovery
reduce
reform
refresh
reject
rejection
rejoice
remains
remark
repair
repeat
reply
reporter
require
respect
respond
restless
restroom
retire
retreat
reveal

revive
ridden
ridge
ringside
rinse
risen
risky
roadwork
roof
roller
rosebud
rotten
rough
route
rowboat
royally
royalty
runny
rut
Ruth

S
sadness
sailor
sake
salesman
salty
Sam
sample
sandwich
sauce
saucepan
saucer
savings
scale
scald
scarecrow
scheme
scold
scoop
scorch
scoreboard
Scotch
Scott
scour
scram
scraper
scratchy
screw
script
scrounge
scruff
search
season
sex
shade
shady
shaken
shaky
shark

she'd
sheer
shelf
shelter
she's
shipwreck
shook
shopping
shore
shortcake
shorts
shove
shown
shyly
side show
sidewalk
sift
sigh
silk
sill
singe
single
sir
skater
sketch
ski
skid
skillful
skinny
skip
skull
slaughter
sled
sleet
sleigh
slept
slid
slide
slight
slot
slouch
slump
smack
smear
Smith
smog
smoky
smooth
smoothly
smudge
snapshot
snarl
snatch
sneak
sneakers
sneaky
sniff
snowball
snowstorm
soar

socks
softly
son
sought
sourball
sourpuss
spaghetti
span
spangle
spark
spear
speck
sped
speech
spendthrift
spin
spine
splurge
spoke
spoken
spoonful
spotless
spout
sprout
spy
squarely
squeaky
squirm
stage fright
stairway
stall
standstill
starch

stash
stem
Steve
Steven
stir
stitch
stocking
stone
stony
stool
stoop
straighten
strain
strap
stray
streak
stress
stressful
strict
struggle
stuffing
stuffy
stunt
stutter
subway
successfully
sue
sugar
sugarless
suit
suitcase
sulk

sulky
sunglasses
sunken
sunless
suppose
surf
swam
Swede
Sweden
sweep
sweeper
swept
swing
Swiss
syllable

T

tag
tailspin
tasteless
tasty
taught
Ted
tee
teepee
teller
tense
Thanksgiving
theft
they're
thickly
thief
thinner

thirst
thirsty
thorn
thread
threat
threaten
thrift
thrifty
throat
throb
throughout
thud
thump
thus
tighten
tightly
tilt
together
toil
Tony
toolbox
toothbrush
toothpaste
tough
trace
trainer
tramp
trance
trashy
tread
trend
tribe

tricky
troop
trooper
trounce
trousers
trout
truce
trudge
truthfully

U

ulcer
unclear
underground
undershirt
understand
unhealthy
unit
uproar

V

van
vane
vanilla
veal
verge
vine
visit
void
volt
vow

W

waist
waistline

waiter
wallet
Walter
waltz
wander
washcloth
washing
wastebasket
watchful
watchman
weaken
weather
wedding
weight

we'll
weren't
whack
wham
wheeze
whether
whichever
whiff
whim
whine
who's
wildly
William
wilt
window
wiring
wise
wisecrack

wisely
woodpecker
woodwork
woody
woolly
workshop
worthless
wrapper
wrapping
wrecker
wren
wrench
wring
wrung

X

Y

yeah
yearly
Y.M.C.A.
yoga
yogurt
you'll
you've
yuk!

Z

Lesson 17

Common Word Beginnings: Part 2

de-	ex-	com-	con-	un-
define	expose	command	conclude	unhealthy
defeat	extend	commander	confess	undo
delight	extent	commandment	confide	undid
devote	extreme	composer	confine	unfit
demand	extremely	composed	conceal	unwilling
decay	express	compare	convince	unlikely
declare	explore	compute	construct	uncover
detach	explorer	comply	conform	uncertain

Words for Study

alarm	figure	booth	hurry
Dennis	desire	whoever	quiet
flu	shopper	comforted	curtain

Tony's Day Off

When the alarm clock rang, Tony shut it off, rolled over, and tried to go back to sleep. He was just about asleep when he remembered that he had to call in sick. If he failed to comply with this rule, his boss would dock him a day's pay. He looked up the number of Mr. Dennis, his boss, in his little black book. The phone rang six times before Mr. Dennis answered it.

"Yeah, what do you want?" said Mr. Dennis in an extremely unfriendly voice.

Tony made his voice sound as weak as he could. "Hi, it's Tony. I think I'm coming down with the flu. Is it okay with you if I take the day off and rest?"

"Who do you think I am, your mother?" exploded Mr. Dennis. "You know very well you've got fifteen sick days a year. If you're sick, you take a sick day. Is that so hard to figure out?"

"I just wanted to check it out," replied Tony, who was having trouble concealing his desire to tell his boss off.

The minute Tony hung up the phone, he felt great. As he took his shower, he made up a little song about Mr. Dennis. The song amused him so much that he cut himself in three places while shaving because he was laughing so hard.

He treated himself to a huge breakfast of grapefruit juice, fried eggs, ham, toast, doughnuts, and coffee at a nearby diner. As he was having his second cup of coffee, he saw an ad in the newspaper for a great clothing sale at a men's store only three blocks from the diner.

It seemed as if every man in town had the same idea because the store was filled with shoppers by the time Tony got there. He had to fight his way to the racks, but he was comforted when he saw how cheap the clothing was compared to other stores in town. He chose two pairs of slacks and a brown sweater to try on.

Tony waited in line to use the fitting booth for what seemed like an hour. "Hey, will you please hurry up in there," commanded Tony. "I haven't got all day, you know."

All at once, it became very quiet in the fitting booth. "Oh, yeah? That's what you think. You'll have all the time in the world to shop for fancy clothes now, Tony," declared Mr. Dennis as he poked his head from behind the curtain, "because you're fired!"

1 **About the Story.** Answer these questions.

1. In what three places does this story take place?

    a. _____

    b. _____

    c. _____

2. Who is Tony's boss? _____

3. What kind of mood is Tony's boss in when Tony calls him up?

    _____

4. Why does Tony say he can't go to work?

    _____

5. What does Tony decide to do after breakfast?

    _____

6. Why does Tony lose his job?

    _____

What do you think?

7. If you were Tony, what would you have said to Mr. Dennis when you saw him in the store?

    _____

    _____

8. Do you think Mr. Dennis will change his mind about firing Tony?

    _____

    _____

2 **More Work with the Sounds for _ow_.** To find the answers, choose a word from **List A** and add a word from **List B** to it.

List A	List B
blow	bowl
dish	down
down	flowers
land	off
low	out
show	owner
snow	people
towns	plow
wash	pour
wild	towel

_____ 1. You use this to dry dishes.

_____ 2. This person owns property.

_____ 3. This word describes something that bursts very quickly, such as an automobile tire.

_____ 4. This is used to remove snow from roads and railroad tracks.

_____ 5. This is a basin that can be filled with water for washing.

_____ 6. These people live in a city or town.

_____ 7. This word describes a heavy rain.

_____ 8. People enjoy picking these on walks through the woods or fields.

_____ 9. This person enjoys doing things that other people notice.

_____ 10. This is a slang term for the whole truth or all the facts about something.

3 **Which Word Does Not Fit?** On the line to the right, write the word that does not fit with the rest.

1. grapefruit	lemon	peach	pear	peas	_____
2. caring	gentle	kind	loving	unfriendly	_____
3. cheek	chin	eyes	knees	mouth	_____
4. brush	comb	lipstick	mirror	purse	_____
5. bold	brave	daring	tough	weak	_____
6. all wet	drenched	dripping	rain	soaked	_____
7. hunted	looked for	searched	shelter	sought	_____
8. go fast	hurry	relax	rush	speed	_____
9. calm	composed	nervous	peaceful	relaxed	_____
10. build	compose	construct	destroy	make	_____
11. conceal	expose	reveal	show	uncover	_____
12. comment	declare	express	mute	speak	_____

4 **More Work with Syllables.** Say each word out loud. On the lines to the right of each word, write the syllables you hear. Study the examples before you begin.

1. confess   _con_ • _fess_

2. booth   _booth_

3. extreme   _ex_ • _treme_

4. extremely   _____ • _____ • _____

5. shopper   _____ • _____

6. flu   _____

7. sixteen   _____ • _____

8. yesterday   _____ • _____ • _____

9. winner   _____ • _____

10. payday   _____ • _____

11. homesick   _____ • _____

12. restroom   _____ • _____

13. overboard   _____ • _____ • _____

14. unfriendly   _____ • _____ • _____

15. basketball   _____ • _____ • _____

Lesson 18

Common Word Beginnings: Part 3

ex-	dis-	un-	im-	in-
exchange	discuss	uncooked	impress	income
exceed	disgust	unlawful	improve	infield
expand	display	unpack	impose	insect
expense	dispose	unpaid	impure	insight
expel	discharge	untrained	import	injure
exist	discover	unafraid	imported	injury
exhaust	discovery	uneven	improper	inquest
exert	disturb	uneasy	improperly	index

Words for Study

admit	limit	garbage	station
you'd	disagree	refrigerator	extra
harsh	hasn't	mention	clippers

A Talk With Jerome

"The trouble with you, Jerome," said Steven, "is that you can't admit you've made a mistake. Instead of just admitting to yourself how much you'd really like to get together with Ginger again and then doing what you have to do in order to get things straightened out, you mope around as if nobody else exists in the universe but you."

Jerome felt that Steven was being too harsh with him, but he was so exhausted from feeling awful that he didn't say a word.

"You know," Steven went on, "there's a limit to just how much you can expect from other people. If you want something bad enough, you're the one who has to go after it. As my mom used to preach to me when I was a kid, the world doesn't owe you anything. And she's right, Jerome. Nobody owes you a thing. It's a hard fact to learn, but it's true."

"I disagree with you there," replied Jerome in a sad voice. "If Ginger wanted to see me, why hasn't she called me up?"

"You're missing the whole point," said Steven who was starting to feel disgusted with the way Jerome refused to face his problem. "The point is that you have to do something to get what you want out of life. Forget all this garbage about what other people should do. That kind of thinking will just drive you crazy. You have to think about what you should be doing for yourself."

"So you think I should call her up?" asked Jerome after a long pause.

"Yeah. If you want to see her, call her up," replied Steven as he went into the kitchen to get himself something to drink.

"What if she doesn't want to see me?" yelled Jerome.

"That's a chance you have to take. The important thing," explained Steven, "is that you'd be doing something instead of waiting around for somebody else to do it for you. Just doing something will make you feel a lot better. Anyway, she must want to see you. Tony told you that she was upset when she found out about your party." Steven was beginning to feel as if he were talking to a child.

"Maybe she was the one who really started the fight with Tony's nutty neighbor just to get out of coming to the party," Jerome said.

Steven slammed the refrigerator door shut in disgust. "Jerome, Tony didn't even mention the party to Ginger until they were driving home from the police station. I really can't talk about this anymore. Either call her up or don't call her up, but don't come complaining to me anymore. I'm sick of it. I just don't want to hear it."

"So why didn't they come to the party after they got out of the police station?" Jerome inquired.

"JEROME! I said I don't want to hear it!"

"Okay, okay," said Jerome.

"Okay, what?" Steven inquired.

"Okay, so I'll call her up!"

1 **About the Story.** Answer these questions.

1. What does Steven think is the matter with Jerome at the beginning of the story?

   _____

   _____

2. What point is Steven trying to get Jerome to understand?

   _____

   _____

3. Why does Jerome think that Ginger might have started the fight with Tony's neighbor?

   _____

   _____

4. Why does Steven get so angry with Jerome?

   _____

5. At the end of the story, does Jerome decide that Steven is right or wrong? How do you know?

   _____

2 **Short Stories.** Fill in the blanks with the right choices from the word groups at the left.

convince
disagreed
discussed
expands
extra

1. In class yesterday, the teacher _____ how water _____ when it is heated. Andy _____ with this, and the teacher spent an _____ ten minutes after class trying to _____ him of the truth of this fact.

2. The policeman pulled Mr. Jones over to the side of the road for _____ the speed limit. The two men _____ angry words. In a very _____ voice, Mr. Jones told the policeman that he was _____ for his job. The policeman hoped the court would fine him an _____ twenty bucks for being so rude.

exceeding
exchanged
extra
unfriendly
unfit

3. Mary was so _____ when she got home from work that she was _____ how long she could keep two jobs and still take care of an apartment and two children. She knew that working this hard was _____, but she had so many _____ that she needed the _____ from two jobs just to make ends meet.

exhausted
expenses
income
uncertain
unhealthy

3 **Who Uses What?** Put the words at the left under the right heading.

bait
boards
boat
cake pans
chair
clippers
combs
dough
drill
hammer
hooks
mirror
nails
net
oven
pie plates
rod
rolling pin
saws
shaving cream

Baker

1. _____

2. _____

3. _____

4. _____

5. _____

Barber

1. _____

2. _____

3. _____

4. _____

5. _____

Carpenter

1. _____

2. _____

3. _____

4. _____

5. _____

Fisherman

1. _____

2. _____

3. _____

4. _____

5. _____

4 **Spelling Check.** The answers to the clues are listed at the left. As you can see, the letters of the words are all mixed up. Spell the words the right way on the lines.

1. b h m t u   _____ Little children suck this when they're upset or bored.

2. A g s t u u   _____ This is the eighth month of the year.

3. a e l l w t   _____ People keep money, snapshots, and important papers in this.

4. a c c e h k p y   _____ A worker gets this each week or every other week for his work.

5. a o o p t t   _____ You can bake, boil, fry, or mash this for your dinner.

6. a C d e e i l l n r   _____ A fairy godmother helped her get to a ball where she waltzed with Prince Charming until the clock struck twelve.

7. a l t w z   _____ This is the kind of dancing that Prince Charming and Answer 6 did at the ball.

8. a a c e e h k p s t   _____ This is a slang term for a person who is really tight with his money.

Lesson 19

Up-, Down-, Out-, Over-, and Under-

up-	down-	out-	over-	under-
update	downhill	outlook	overgrown	undershirt
upstate	downfall	outcome	overhead	underground
uproar	downright	outdoors	overtime	underdog
uptown	downstream	outsmart	overnight	understood
upkeep	downpour	outskirts	overcome	undertaker
upstairs	downstairs	outfield	overflow	underwear
upside-down	downhearted	outstanding	overseas	underneath
upcoming	down-to-earth	outnumber	overweight	underworld

Words for Study

nightclub	beauty	September
weekday	intense	subject
somewhat	chilly	bouncer

Jerome and Ginger

Jerome decided that he would not call Ginger after all. He would go see her in person. Checking through the newspaper, he saw that Ginger was singing at a nightclub that had just opened uptown. As he was putting on his overcoat, he found himself humming one of the first songs that Ginger had ever written. Steven had been right. Now that Jerome had decided to act, he no longer felt downhearted.

Jerome got to the club at about eleven o'clock. Because it was a weekday night, the crowd was very small. A waiter sat him at a table just to the right of the band. Ginger, who wasn't singing at the time, was sitting next to the piano player. Jerome had forgotten just how lovely she was. In spite of the fact that she looked tired and somewhat bored, Ginger's charm and beauty put her in a class all by herself.

She must have felt Jerome's stare; for at that very moment, she looked up from the keyboard and gazed right into Jerome's eyes. It would have been clear to anybody who happened to be watching that both Ginger and Jerome were overcome with intense feelings. Ginger murmured something into the piano player's ear, got up, and walked slowly over to Jerome's table.

"Hello, Jerome," she said shyly.

"Hi, Ginger." Jerome's voice was just as shy. "How have you been?"

"I'm okay. What brought you up here on this dark, chilly night?" Ginger asked.

"Oh, I just felt like hearing 'September Song' and I didn't have any plans for this evening, so I thought I'd just come on up here and ask you to sing it for me," Jerome lied.

"You always said that 'September Song' made you want to throw up!" exclaimed Ginger.

"Ginger! Don't be so crude!"

"Why not? You always said that people should never beat around the bush which is exactly what I think you're doing right now."

"Can I buy you a drink, or do you get them free here?" asked Jerome quickly.

"I get them free," Ginger responded, "and don't change the subject."

"Okay. Are you going to sing 'September Song?'"

"Jerome," threatened Ginger. "I'm going to give you just one more chance to explain what you're doing here, and then I'm going to tell the bouncer to throw you out on your ear."

"You have gotten crude," teased Jerome.

"Life is tough. What can I say?" Ginger glanced around the room to see where the bouncer was.

"Well, you've just answered your own question," said Jerome slowly.

"What do you mean by that?"

"I mean," said Jerome, who was looking straight into Ginger's eyes now, "that life is tough. Things haven't been going very well for me. And underneath all my crazy clowning around, I miss you very much."

Ginger said nothing. She touched Jerome gently on the cheek and turned to go back to the band. "Hey!" shouted Jerome. "I'm sorry! Where are you going?"

"To sing 'September Song,'" she replied softly. "Just make sure you don't throw up."

1 **About the Story.** Answer these questions.

1. Why does Jerome decide not to call up Ginger?

   _____

2. Where does most of this story take place?

   _____

3. What is Ginger doing when Jerome first sees her?

   _____

4. What reason does Jerome first give Ginger for coming to see her?

   _____

5. What does Ginger threaten to do?

   _____

6. How do you know that Ginger is very happy to see Jerome again?

   _____

2 **The Months of the Year.** Do you remember this verse?

> Thirty days has September,
> April, June, and November.
> When short February is done,
> All the rest have thirty-one.

Use the list of months to fill in the blanks. You may need to use a word more than once.

January

February

March

April

May

June

July

August

September

October

November

December

1. In what month is New Year's Day?

2. In what month is New Year's Eve?

3. In what month is Christmas?

4. In what month is Thanksgiving?

5. In what month is George Washington's birthday?

6. In what month is your birthday?

7. In what month do most children return to school?

8. In what month do most children get out of school?

9. In what month does spring begin?

10. In what month does summer begin?

11. In what month does autumn begin?

12. In what month does winter begin?

13. Which month of the year do you like the most?

14. Which month of the year do you like the least?

3 **The Four Seasons.** Put each word at the left under the best heading.

	Spring	Summer
April	1. _____	1. _____
August	2. _____	2. _____
beach	3. _____	3. _____
Christmas	4. _____	4. _____
December		
Easter		
falling leaves		
flowers blooming		
Fourth of July	**Autumn**	**Winter**
ice skating		
October	1. _____	1. _____
schools open		
snowstorms	2. _____	2. _____
spring training	3. _____	3. _____
Thanksgiving		
the All-Star game	4. _____	4. _____

4 **Twelve Questions.** Write the underlined word that is right on the line to the left.

_____ 1. In most houses, are the bedrooms <u>downstairs</u> or <u>upstairs</u>?

_____ 2. If it's raining hard outside, do children play <u>indoors</u> or <u>outdoors</u>?

_____ 3. Does the pitcher in a baseball game stand in the <u>infield</u> or the <u>outfield</u>?

_____ 4. Is the money that you earn called your <u>income</u> or your <u>outcome</u>?

_____ 5. When you take out the trash, are you <u>composing</u> or <u>disposing</u> of it?

_____ 6. If you broil a steak for a long time, is it <u>overdone</u> or <u>underdone</u>?

_____ 7. When you feel very happy with your life, are you <u>content</u> or <u>intent</u>?

_____ 8. If you have just been invited to a neighborhood party, do you feel <u>included</u> or <u>excluded</u>?

_____ 9. If somebody makes a mistake and you know it but don't say anything, do you <u>outlook</u> it or <u>overlook</u> it?

_____ 10. If you tell your boss that you refuse to do something that you've been ordered to do, are you <u>complying</u> or <u>replying</u>?

_____ 11. When you ask for something, is this an <u>inquest</u> or a <u>request</u>?

_____ 12. If you want to let some of the air out of your automobile tires, do you <u>deflate</u> or <u>inflate</u> them?

Lesson 20

More Work with Compound Words

bookstore	widespread	teaspoon	blacksmith
bookmark	bedspread	tablespoon	blackmail
landmark	bedtime	tablecloth	slowpoke
landlord	mealtime	clothesline	slowdown
landlady	Passover	clothespin	sundown
homeland	password	hairpin	sunrise
homebody	passport	hairbrush	heartbeat
housework	seaport	paintbrush	heartbreak
courthouse	seacoast	horseback	breakdown
farmhouse	seafood	horseplay	breakthrough

Words for Study

contract	beautiful	midnight	honor
tomato	dessert	different	content
arrived	including	Jews	shoulder

Holly Gives a Party

Holly was giving a huge party. She had just signed a contract that morning for her book, and the president of the firm had told her that her health food cookbook would be on the shelves of all the well-known bookstores and health food stores by February.

She had invited the whole yoga class, Gail, Jerome and Ginger, Tony, and a few other friends. Because Steven had been so helpful in testing the recipes, she told him to go ahead and invite anybody else he wanted to be there.

When Jerome called Holly to thank her for inviting him, he asked her if she were going to serve real food like spaghetti and meat balls and French bread and chocolate cake. Holly just laughed and told him that she was so sick of all the recipes in her cookbook that she had already planned to have a spaghetti dinner. "In that case," said Jerome, "you can count on me to help with the dishes. Can I bring anything?"

"Bring some wine," Holly replied. "And, if you don't mind, call Tony and tell him to bring some, too. I've got to start making the tomato sauce right now if everything is going to be ready on time."

The party was a great success. Ginger hadn't arrived yet, but she was planning to come just as soon as she got off from work. Holly looked beautiful in a red dress that she had rushed out to buy between making the tomato sauce and baking the cheesecake. Everyone was happy for her success as a cookbook writer.

Jerome decided that if Ginger ever left him again, he would fall in love with Holly (now that he knew she made great spaghetti). But he understood deep in his heart that, in spite of any rough times that were sure to come, he and Ginger would be together for a long, long time.

Just as a gag, Holly brought out a large glass bowl of prune whip for dessert. Some of the people from the yoga class were delighted; but most of the guests, including Steven, turned pale and wondered if Holly's feelings would be hurt if they refused to eat it.

"Just a joke," grinned Holly. "The real desserts are in the kitchen."

"Now I know why they call a gag, a gag," Steven remarked, looking at the awful prune whip.

Ginger arrived at Holly's apartment about midnight because she had been able to leave work early. Ginger had never met Holly before, and the two women liked each other at once. Ginger also enjoyed meeting all the people from the yoga class and asked all sorts of questions about yoga.

Jerome could tell from how excited Ginger was that, by next week, both he and Ginger would be down at the Y.M.C.A. trying to stand on their heads. He didn't mind. He remembered his own party and how bad he had felt. It all seemed like a long time ago, even though it really wasn't. Now, here he was, feeling so happy, with Ginger by his side and his third plate of chocolate cheesecake in his hand.

"That's life," he thought to himself as he kissed Ginger on the cheek. "One minute you're down, and the next minute you're up. You just never know what's going to happen next!"

1 **About the Story.** Answer these questions.

1. Why is Holly giving a party?

_____

2. What did Jerome ask Holly when he called her to thank her for inviting him?

_____

3. Why has Holly planned to serve exactly what Jerome wants to eat?

_____

4. At what time does Ginger get to the party? _____

5. Why is she late? _____

6. What does Holly serve for dessert as a gag? _____

7. What is the real dessert? _____

8. What does Ginger think of the people from the yoga class?

_____

9. How does Jerome seem different in this story?

_____

10. What does Jerome seem to have learned about life?

_____

_____

2 **More Work with Compound Words.** Choose the right word from the four choices and write it on the line to the left.

_____ 1. Sometimes you have to show this paper in order to pass from one country into another.
(a) passbook   (b) Passover   (c) passport   (d) password

_____ 2. This is the time when the Jews honor the flight of the Jews from Egypt, which is recorded in the second book of the Bible.
(a) passbook   (b) Passover   (c) passport   (d) password

_____ 3. This person is most content when he is in his own home.
(a) anybody   (b) busybody   (c) homebody   (d) somebody

_____ 4. This is a knapsack that is worn on the back to carry camping gear.

   (a) background   (b) backpack   (c) backtrack   (d) backwoods

_____ 5. This is another word for your spine.

   (a) backbone   (b) backfire   (c) backrest   (d) backside

_____ 6. This is an unsafe building, or one that would be hard to get out of if there were a fire.

   (a) firecracker   (b) firelight   (c) fireplace   (d) firetrap

_____ 7. This word describes a person's hands that are rough and red from having been in water so much.

   (a) dishpan   (b) dishrag   (c) dishtowel   (d) dishwater

_____ 8. This is the lower half of the leg of a cooked chicken. It's also used for beating a drum.

   (a) chopstick   (b) dipstick   (c) drumstick   (d) lipstick

_____ 9. Three of these make one tablespoon.

   (a) teacups   (b) teapots   (c) tearooms   (d) teaspoons

_____ 10. These are loose-fitting trousers with a bib front and shoulder straps.

   (a) overall   (b) overalls   (c) overcoat   (d) overdraw

3 **Words That Mean the Same.** Choose the word from the line that means the same thing as the first word and write it on the line to the right. Study the example before you begin.

1. **discover:**	conceal	cover	find	lose	_find_
2. **exhausted:**	asleep	relaxed	starving	tired	_____
3. **heavy:**	slim	skinny	overweight	thin	_____
4. **barely:**	hardly	loosely	not at all	unlikely	_____
5. **thrown:**	baseball	caught	harmed	hurled	_____
6. **harsh:**	calm	mild	rough	rude	_____
7. **spear:**	crowbar	knife	lance	scraper	_____
8. **drift:**	retreat	slide	toil	wander	_____
9. **scorch:**	singe	smudge	sprout	struggle	_____
10. **sulk:**	plead	pout	praise	prance	_____

4 **Word Opposites.** Choose the word from the line that means the opposite of the first word and write it on the line to the right. Study the example before you begin.

1. **male:**	grandmother	daughter	female	lady	*female*
2. **sweet:**	awful	honey	sour	sugar	
3. **evening:**	afternoon	dawn	dusk	morning	
4. **chill:**	cool	freeze	heat	icy	
5. **thaw:**	freeze	liquid	melt	solid	
6. **dash:**	crawl	dart	hurry	rush	
7. **rare:**	burned	common	odd	strange	
8. **excited:**	asleep	bored	content	relaxed	
9. **not sure:**	deserved	certain	dumb	square	
10. **expand:**	conform	conclude	confide	contract	

5 **Feelings.** How do you think the people in these little stories feel? Choose your answer from the four choices and write it on the line. Then, on the line below the story, explain why you have picked this answer.

1. When the fans saw the shortstop on the other team get thrown out of the game for repeated

swearing, they _____.

(a) cheered   (c) sighed
(b) jeered   (d) smiled

_____

2. Joan read an ad in the newspaper that described just the kind of job she had always dreamed

of having. Joan felt _____.

(a) excited   (c) tense
(b) scared   (d) unhappy

_____

3. Roy had just lost his last quarter in the Coke machine. Roy was _____.

(a) angry   (c) pleasant
(b) cool   (d) thrifty

_____

4. When Charles was informed he had just won fifty thousand dollars, tears ran down

   his cheeks. Charles was _____.
   (a) angry   (c) downhearted
   (b) calm   (d) overcome with feeling

5. John learned that his neighbor was having a party, and everybody else in the neighborhood

   had been invited. John felt _____.
   (a) calm   (c) okay
   (b) mad   (d) rejected

6. Ted just hated his boss, but he loved his job. When he was told that his boss was planning

   to move to Boston, he was _____.
   (a) calm   (c) happy
   (b) grouchy   (d) nervous

7. When the police phoned Mrs. Martin and told her that they had found her son and

   that he was all right, she felt _____.
   (a) disturbed   (c) mistreated
   (b) happy   (d) thankful

8. You have just completed the last lesson in the third reading book.

   How do you feel? _____
   (a) downhearted   (c) wiped out
   (b) joyful   (d) ready to start Book 4

Review: Lessons 1-20 ━━━━━━━━━━

1 **Word Study.** Put the letter of the best answer on the line to the left of the sentence.

_____ 1. John *intended* to call his brother as soon as he got home from work. *Intend* means _____.

   (a) to confront
   (b) to insist
   (c) to plan
   (d) to wonder

_____ 2. The actors always had *stage fright* just before the curtain went up.

   (a) The actors wanted people to enjoy their acting.
   (b) The actors were edgy.
   (c) The actors forgot all their lines.
   (d) The actors needed help getting dressed for the play.

_____ 3. By the time Dan got from the driveway to the front porch, he was *drenched*. *Drenched* means _____.

   (a) confused
   (b) exhausted
   (c) ready for dinner
   (d) soaked

_____ 4. Mr. Gray always felt *gloomy* just before and right after his birthday. *Gloomy* means _____.

   (a) downhearted
   (b) excited
   (c) relaxed
   (d) tense

_____ 5. The Cowboys *trounced* the Colts in yesterday's football game. The Cowboys _____.

   (a) barely won the game
   (b) beat the Colts badly
   (c) lost the game
   (d) lost the game by quite a few touchdowns

_____ 6. The doctors believed they were on the *verge* of discovering a cure for cancer.

   (a) They felt many more years of study would have to take place.
   (b) They felt they were about to make an important breakthrough.
   (c) They needed more money for the tests they were doing in their labs.
   (d) They thought things were hopeless.

_____ 7. Mr. Smith read *Consumer Reports* to learn more about which refrigerators were rated as the best buys. A *consumer* is someone who _____.

   (a) buys goods
   (b) cannot afford to spend more than he has to
   (c) likes to own the best that money can buy
   (d) needs advice about how he should spend his money

_____ 8. Paul *murmured* to his wife that he thought they should leave the party early.

   (a) He sent a note.
   (b) He spoke loudly.
   (c) He spoke softly.
   (d) He stuttered.

_____ 9. Ruth decided to take a few things out of her knapsack, so it would be easier to carry on the hike. The knapsack was probably too _____.

   (a) bulky
   (b) costly
   (c) faulty
   (d) knotty

_____ 10. The speaker *concluded* his talk with a joke about people who fail to file their income tax returns. *Conclude* means _____.

   (a) to begin
   (b) to break up
   (c) to end
   (d) to halt

_____ 11. When the manager informed the workers that they would not get their yearly raise, no one *uttered* a word. *Utter* means _____.

   (a) to demand
   (b) to defend
   (c) to include
   (d) to speak

_____ 12. Cases of flu are *widespread* during the winter months. *Widespread* means _____.

   (a) common
   (b) costly
   (c) disturbing
   (d) painful

_____ 13. Mr. Bloom was thought of as a *bigwig* by all the townspeople.

   (a) He was a very important person.
   (b) He was known by most of the townspeople.
   (c) He worked for the town.
   (d) He was bald.

_____ 14. Joan's first thought when she looked at the apartment was it had a very *homey* look. Joan thought that the apartment was _____.

   (a) cheap
   (b) fair
   (c) pleasant
   (d) well-done

_____ 15. When the teacher asked the class who invented the light bulb, Jill *blurted* out the answer.

   (a) She gave the wrong answer.
   (b) She guessed the answer and was right.
   (c) She refused to give the answer.
   (d) She spoke before she was called upon to give the answer.

2 **Words That Mean the Same.** Match the word at the left with the word at the right that means the same.

beg	_____	1. faithful
content		
fib	_____	2. grouchy
fussy	_____	3. jumpy
grab		
hoist	_____	4. lie
loyal		
nervous	_____	5. needy
pledge	_____	6. plead
poor		
	_____	7. pleased
	_____	8. raise
	_____	9. snatch
	_____	10. vow

3 **Word Opposites.** Match the word at the left with the word at the right that means the opposite.

complex

costly   _____   1. crooked

fancy   _____   2. dirty

loosen   _____   3. expand

phony

quiet   _____   4. noisy

shrink   _____   5. overhead

spotless

straight   _____   6. plain

underneath   _____   7. simple

              _____   8. tighten

              _____   9. truthful

              _____   10. worthless

4 **Syllables.** Say each word out loud. On the lines to the right of each word, write the syllables you hear.

1. cloudless   _____ • _____

2. successful   _____ • _____ • _____

3. robber   _____ • _____

4. sideways   _____ • _____

5. thirteen   _____ • _____

6. thoughtful   _____ • _____

7. retire   _____ • _____

8. handshake   _____ • _____

9. sitter   _____ • _____

10. peacefully _____ • _____ • _____

5 **Word Sounds.** Choose the word in each line that has a different underlined sound. Write this word on the line to the right. Study the examples before you begin.

1. bl<u>a</u>de   r<u>a</u>nge   w<u>a</u>ke   w<u>a</u>lk   _walk_

2. <u>c</u>atch   <u>c</u>ity   <u>c</u>ode   <u>c</u>ome   _city_

3. <u>g</u>ame   <u>g</u>entle   <u>g</u>irl   <u>g</u>oal   _____

4. b<u>ea</u>t   gr<u>ea</u>t   l<u>ea</u>st   m<u>ea</u>l   _____

5. b<u>oo</u>th   g<u>oo</u>d   g<u>oo</u>se   r<u>oo</u>f   _____

6. b<u>ow</u>l   <u>ow</u>n   pl<u>ow</u>   sn<u>ow</u>   _____

7. bl<u>ou</u>se   c<u>ou</u>ld   p<u>ou</u>nd   sh<u>ou</u>t   _____

8. <u>ai</u>m   cert<u>ai</u>n   m<u>ai</u>l   w<u>ai</u>st   _____

6 **Spelling Check.** The answers to the clues are listed at the left. As you can see, the letters are all mixed up. Spell the words the right way on the lines. HINT: When you are done, the first letter of each answer, reading down, spells the name of a dessert.

1. c m o o o r r t u   _____ This is where you can find a judge and jury.

2. a g h h i w y   _____ This is where you can find lots of automobiles being driven home, to work, etc.

3. a d E g l n n   _____ This is where you find people who speak English.

4. e e g g h l l s   _____ This is where you can find a baby chick before it has hatched.

5. c h l o o s   _____ This is where you can go to take a course if you want to learn about something.

6. a e r   _____ This is where you put an earring.

7. b c k k o o o o   _____ This is where you look if you want to find a new recipe to try out on your family or friends.

8. a a h r s t y   _____ This is where you put your ashes if you're smoking in someone's home.

9. c e h i k n t   _____ This is where you use the answer to Question 7. (It's a room in your house.)

10. E l a D d o o r   _____ This is where men thought they could find lots of gold. It's also the name of a fancy automobile.

What is the name of the dessert that the first letters of each answer, reading down, spell?

— — — — — — — — — —

gentleman
gently
given
glance
globe
gloom
gloomy
glove
glow
gnarled
gnash
gnat
gnaw
gnawing
gnome
gob
gobble
godmother
golly
goo
goof
goofy
gorge
gosh
grab
grace
grain
grandfather
grandmother
grapefruit
grease
Greece
greedy
Greek
greet
grill
grind
grouchy
growl
grownup
grudge
gulf
gull
gully
gulp
gumdrop
gust
gut
gutter

H

hairbrush
haircut
hairpin
hairy
half
halt
handshake
happiness
hardware

harp
harsh
Harvey
hasn't
haul
haunt
haunted
headquarters
health
healthy
heart
heartbeat
heartbreak
height
hem
herb
Herb
highness
highway
hiss
hoist
holder
Holly
homebody
homeland
homemade
homesick
homey
honor
horseback
horseplay
hotel
hourglass
hourly
housewife
housework
how's
huh
hurl
hurry

I

icing
import
imported
impose
impress
improper
improperly
improve
impure
include
income
increase
index
indoors
infect
infield
inflate
inform

inhale
injure
injury
inquest
inquire
insect
inside
insight
insist
inspire
instruct
intend
intense
intent
invade
invent
invite
involve
ivy

J

jeer
Jello
jelly
Jerome
jet
Jew
Joyce
joyful
judge
juice
juicy
jumpy
jury

K

keg
keyboard
kin
kinfolk
Kirk
kitchen
knack
knapsack
kneecap
knelt
knickknack
knight
knob
knockout
knot
knotty

L

lance
landlady
landlord
landmark
landowner
lard
lately
laughter
laundromat

laundry
lawyer
lazy
leaky
leap
leapfrog
leash
leather
ledge
Lee
lemon
lesson
library
lifeguard
lighten
lighthouse
limit
lining
listen
lively
lodge
longing
loose
loosen
lousy
lowdown
lower
loyally
loyalty
Luke
lukewarm
lunge
lurch

M

machine
madly
mailbox
mailman
mall
malt
mankind
Mansfield
Martin
mash
matchbook
Matthew
mealtime
meatball
mention
merge
midnight
might
mildly
mince
mincemeat
miscount
misjudge
misplace
misspell

mist
mistaken
mistreat
mistrust
moan
moist
moisten
mold
moldy
moment
moose
mope
motel
murder
murmur

N

nasty
naughty
nearby
neatly
neighbor
neighborhood
neither
nervous
newspaper
newsstand
New Year's Eve
nightclub
noisy
nonsense
nook
noose
nor
Norway
notch
notice
November
nudge

O

oak
oat
oatmeal
October
oddly
oh
onto
ooze
ought
ours
ourselves
outcome
outdoors
outfield
outlook
outnumber
outskirts
outsmart
outstanding
overall
overalls

overboard
overcoat
overcome
overdraw
overflow
overgrown
overhead
overlook
overnight
overseas
overtime
overweight
owe
owner
ox

P

pact
padding
painful
painless
paintbrush
palm
pane
passbook
Passover
passport
password
paste
patty
Paul
pause
pave
paving
peaceful
peacefully
peanut
peeler
perch
perk
phony
piano
pickle
piece
pigpen
pill
pillow
pinch
pitch
pitcher
pitchfork
plainly
playground
plea
plead
pleasant
pleased
pledge
plenty
plow
plump

plunge
poach
poorhouse
poorly
porch
potato
potato chip
pounce
pout
practice
praise
prance
press
pretty
prince
probably
prop
proper
properly
property
proudly
pry
puffy
putty

Q

quarter
quarterback
quiet

R

rag
raft
railroad
rainy
rarely
rash
rear
recall
recipe
recover
recovery
reduce
reform
refresh
refrigerator
reject
rejection
rejoice
remains
remark
repair
repeat
reply
reporter
request
require
respect
respond
restless
restroom

retire
retreat
reveal
revive
ridden
ridge
ringside
rinse
risen
risky
roadwork
roller
roof
rosebud
rotten
rough
route
rowboat
royally
royalty
runny
rut
Ruth

S

sadness
sailor
sake
salesman
salty
Sam
sample
sandwich
sauce
saucepan
saucer
savings
scale
scald
scarecrow
scheme
scold
scoop
scorch
scoreboard
Scotch
Scott
scour
scram
scraper
scratchy
screw
script
scrounge
scruff
seacoast
seafood
seaport
search
season
September

sex
shade
shady
shaken
shaky
shark
she'd
sheer
shelf
shelter
she's
shipwreck
shook
shopper
shopping
shore
shortcake
shorts
shoulder
shove
showoff
shown
shyly
side show
sidewalk
sift
sigh
silk
sill
singe
single
sir
skater
sketch
ski
skid
skillful
skinny
skip
skull
slaughter
sled
sleet
sleigh
slept
slid
slide
slight
slot
slouch
slowdown
slowpoke
slump
smack
smear
Smith
smog
smoky
smooth
smoothly

smudge
snapshot
snarl
snatch
sneak
sneakers
sneaky
sniff
snowball
snowplow
snowstorm
soar
socks
softly
somewhat
son
sought
sourball
sourpuss
spaghetti
span
spangle
spark
spear
speck
sped
speech
spendthrift
spin
spine
splurge
spoke
spoken
spoonful
spotless
spout
sprout
spy
squarely
squeaky
squirm
stage fright
stairway
stall
standstill
starch
stash
station
stem
Steve
Steven
stir
stitch
stocking
stone
stony
stool
stoop
straighten
strain

strap
stray
streak
stress
stressful
strict
struggle
stuffing
stuffy
stunt
stutter
subject
subway
successfully
sue
sugar
sugarless
suit
suitcase
sulk
sulky
sundown
sunglasses
sunken
sunless
sunrise
suppose
surf
swam
Swede
Sweden
sweep
sweeper
swept
swing
Swiss
syllable

T

table
tablecloth
tablespoon
tag
tailspin
tasteless
tasty
taught
teacup
teapot
tearoom
teaspoon
Ted
tee
teepee
teller
tense
Thanksgiving
theft
they're
thickly

thief
thinner
thirst
thirsty
thorn
thread
threat
threaten
thrift
thrifty
throat
throb
throughout
thud
thump
thus
tighten
tightly
tilt
together
toil
tomato
Tony
toolbox
toothbrush
toothpaste
tough
townspeople
trace
trainer
tramp
trance
trashy
tread
trend
tribe
tricky
troop
trooper
trounce
trousers
trout
truce
trudge
truthfully

U

ulcer
unafraid
uncertain
unclear
uncooked
uncover
underdog
underdone
underground
underneath
undershirt
understand
understood

undertaker
underwear
underworld
undid
undo
uneasy
uneven
unfit
unhealthy
unit
unlawful
unlikely
unpack
unpaid
untrained
unwilling
upcoming
update
upkeep
uproar
upside-down
upstairs
upstate
uptown

V

van
vane
vanilla
veal
verge
vine
visit
void
volt
vow

W

waist
waistline
waiter
wallet
Walter
waltz
wander
washbowl
washcloth
washing
wastebasket
watchful
watchman
weaken
weather
wedding
weekday
weight
we'll
weren't
whack
wham
wheeze

whether
whichever
whiff
whim
whine
whoever
who's
widespread
wildflower
wildly
William
wilt
window
wiring
wise
wisecrack
wisely
woodpecker
woodwork
woody
woolly
workshop
worthless
wrapper
wrapping
wrecker
wren
wrench
wring
wrung

X

Y

yeah
yearly
Y.M.C.A.
yoga
yogurt
you'd
you'll
you've
yuk!

Z

Word Index: Books 1-3

a
able
about
above
according
ace
across
act
actor
ad
add
admit
advice
afford
afraid
after
afternoon
afterward
again
against
age
ago
agree
ahead
ahoy
aid
ail
aim
air
alarm
alive
all
allow
all right
all-star
almost
alone
along
alphabet
already
also
although
always
am
amuse
amusement
an
and
Andy
anger
angry
animal
Ann(e)
another
answer
ant
any

anybody
anymore
anything
anyway
anywhere
apart
apartment
ape
April
are
aren't
arm
armchair
armful
army
around
arrive
art
as
ash
ashtray
ask
asleep
at
ate
August
aunt
auto
automobile
autumn
avoid
awake
away
awful
awoke
baby
babysit
babysitter
back
backbone
backfire
background
backpack
backrest
backside
backtrack
backwoods
bad
badge
badly
bag
bail
bait
bake
baker
bald
ball

band
bang
bank
banker
banner
bar
barbed
barber
bare
barely
barge
bark
barn
Bart
base
baseball
basin
basket
basketball
bat
batch
bath
bathe
bathing
bathroom
bathtub
batter
battle
B.C.
be
beach
bead
bean
bear
beard
beast
beat
beaten
beautiful
beauty
became
because
become
bed
bedding
bedroom
bedspread
bedtime
bee
beef
been
beep
beer
beet
before
beg
began

begin
beginner
begun
behave
behind
believe
bell
belong
below
belt
Ben
bench
bend
bender
bent
berserk
beside
besides
best
bet
better
between
bib
Bible
bid
big
bigwig
bike
bill
billfold
billion
Billy
bin
bind
binge
bingo
birch
bird
birth
birthday
bit
bitch
bite
bitten
bitter
black
blackbird
blackboard
blackmail
blacksmith
blacktop
blade
blame
blank
blast
bleach
bleed

blend
bless
blessing
blew
blind
blindly
blink
blob
block
blood
bloodstream
bloody
bloom
blouse
blow
blowout
blown
blue
blues
bluff
blurt
blush
board
boarder
boardwalk
boast
boat
Bob
Bobby
bobsled
body
bodyguard
boil
boiler
bold
bolt
bomb
bond
bone
bony
book
bookcase
bookmark
bookshelf
bookstore
bookworm
boom
boot
booth
booty
booze
bop
border
bore
born
boss
bossy

Boston
both
bought
bounce
bouncer
bouncy
bound
bow
bowl
bowling
box
boxer
boy
Boy Scout
brace
bracelet
brag
braid
brain
brainy
brake
branch
brand
brand-new
brave
bravely
bread
break
breakdown
breakfast
breakthrough
breast
breath
breathe
breathing
breathless
breed
breeze
brew
bribe
brick
bride
bridge
bright
brightly
bring
brink
broil
broke
broken
brook
broom
brother
brotherly
brought
brown
brownie

bruise
brush
buck
Bucky
bud
buddy
bug
buggy
build
building
bulb
bulk
bulky
bull
bum
bump
bumper
bumpy
bun
bunch
bunk
bunt
burn
burner
burp
burst
bus
bush
busily
business
bust
busy
busybody
but
butch
butter
buy
buzz
by
cab
cage
cake
California
call
calm
calmly
came
camp
camper
camping
can
cancer
candy
cane
cannot
can't
cap

cape
Cape Cod
car
card
cardboard
care
careful
careless
carpenter
carpet
carry
cart
carve
case
cash
cast
cat
catbird
catcall
catch
catcher
catfish
catty
caught
cause
caution
cautious
cave
ceiling
celebrate
cell
cellar
cent
center
certain
certainly
chain
chair
chalk
chalkboard
chance
change
charge
Charles
charm
chart
chase
cheap
cheaply
cheapskate
cheat
check
checkbook
checkers
cheek
cheer
cheerful
Cheerios

cheerleader
cheery
cheese
cheesecake
chess
chessboard
chest
chestnut
chew
chick
chicken
child
children
chill
chilly
chin
chip
chirp
chocolate
choice
choke
choose
chop
chopstick
chore
choose
chosen
chow
Christ
Christian
Christmas
chrome
chunk
church
cider
cigar
cigarette
cinch
cinder
Cinderella
circle
circus
city
claim
clam
clap
Clark
clash
class
classroom
claw
clay
clean
cleaner
clear
clearing
clench

clerk
click
cliff
climb
clip
clippers
clipping
clock
close
cloth
clothes
clothesline
clothespin
clothing
cloud
cloudless
cloudy
clown
club
clue
clung
clutch
clutter
coach
coal
coast
coaster
coat
cob
cobweb
cock
cockroach
cocky
cocoa
coconut
cod
code
coffee
coffeecake
coil
coin
Coke
cold
cold-blooded
colt
comb
combine
come
comeback
comfort
coming
command
commander
commandment
comment
commit
common

commonly
compare
compete
complain
complaint
complete
completely
complex
comply
compose
composed
composer
compound
compute
computer
conceal
concern
concert
conclude
cone
confess
confide
confine
conform
confront
confuse
consent
consonant
construct
consume
consumer
contain
container
content
contract
control
convict
convince
cook
cookbook
cool
cop
cope
copper
copy
copycat
cord
cork
corn
corner
cornstarch
corny
corpse
cost
costly
cot
couch

cough
could
couldn't
count
counter
countless
country
countrymen
course
court
courthouse
courtroom
cousin
cove
cover
covering
cow
cowboy
crack
cracker
cramp
crane
crash
crate
crawl
crazy
cream
creep
creepy
crew
crib
crime
crook
crooked
crop
cross
crosswalk
crouch
crow
crowbar
crowd
crown
crude
cruise
cruiser
crumb
crunch
crush
crust
crutch
cry
crybaby
cub
cube
cud
cuff
cup
cupboard

cupcake
cupful
curb
cure
curl
curse
curtain
curve
cut
cute
cutters
cutting
dab
dad
daddy
daily
dam
damp
Dan
dance
dancer
danger
dare
dark
darn
dart
dash
date
daughter
Dave
dawn
day
daybreak
daydream
dead
deadline
deadly
deal
dear
death
debate
decay
December
decide
deck
declare
deed
deep
deer
defeat
defend
define
deflate
delight
demand
den
Dennis

dense
dent
dentist
depend
describe
deserve
desire
desk
dessert
destroy
detach
Detroit
devote
dice
Dick
did
diddle
didn't
die
difference
different
dig
dill
dim
dime
dine
diner
dinner
dip
dipper
dipstick
dirt
dirty
disagree
discharge
discover
discovery
discuss
disgust
dish
dishpan
dishrag
dishtowel
dishwater
display
dispose
disturb
ditch
dive
diver
do
dock
doctor
dodge
does
doesn't
dog

doggy
dollar
dome
done
donkey
don't
door
doorbell
doorknob
doorman
doormat
doorway
dope
dose
dot
double
dough
doughnut
down
downfall
downhearted
downhill
downpour
downright
downstairs
downstream
down-to-earth
downtown
doze
Dr.
drag
drain
drank
drape
draw
drawn
dread
dreadful
dream
dreamer
dreamland
drench
dress
dresser
dressing
drew
drift
drill
drink
drip
drive
driven
driver
driveway
drone
drop
drove

drown
drug
drugstore
drum
drumstick
drunk
dry
dryer
duck
due
dues
dug
duke
dull
dumb
dummy
dump
dunce
dune
dunk
during
dusk
dust
Dutch
each
ear
early
earn
earring
earth
east
Easter
easy
eat
eaten
Eddie
edge
edgy
eel
egg
egghead
eggshell
Egypt
eight
eighteen
eighth
eighty
either
elbow
El Dorado
eleven
elf
elk
elm
else
employer
empty

end
ending
England
English
enjoy
enough
enter
etc.
eve
even
evening
ever
every
everybody
everyone
everything
everywhere
exact
exactly
example
exceed
except
exchange
excite
exclaim
exclude
excuse
exercise
exert
exhaust
exist
expand
expect
expel
expense
expert
explain
explode
explore
explorer
expose
express
ex-slave
extend
extent
extra
extreme
extremely
eye
eyesight
eyestrain
face
fact
factor
fad
fade
fail

faint
fair
fairly
fairness
fairy
faith
faithful
fake
fall
fallen
false
fame
family
fan
fancy
fang
far
fare
farm
farmer
farmhouse
farther
fast
fat
fate
father
faucet
fault
faulty
fear
feast
feather
February
fed
fee
feed
feel
feeling
feet
fell
felt
female
fence
fetch
few
fib
fiddle
fiddler
field
fifteen
fifty
fig
fight
fighter
figure
file
fill

film
filter
fin
find
fine
finger
fingernail
fingerprint
fir
fire
firecracker
firelight
fireplace
firetrap
firm
firmly
first
fish
fisherman
fist
fit
fitting
five
fix
flag
flake
flaky
flame
flap
flare
flash
flashlight
flat
flea
fleet
flesh
flew
flight
flip
flirt
float
flock
flood
floor
flop
flour
flow
flower
flowerpot
flu
flush
flute
fly
fog
foggy
foil
fold

folder
folk
folks
fond
food
fool
foot
football
footprint
for
forbid
force
forefeet
forge
forget
forgetful
forgive
forgiven
forgot
forgotten
fork
form
forth
forty
forty-niner
forward
fought
found
four
fourteen
fourth
Fourth of July
fox
frame
France
freak
free
freedom
freeway
freeze
freezer
freight
French
fresh
freshly
freshman
Friday
friend
friendly
fright
frighten
frog
from
front
froze
frozen
fruit

fruitcake
fry
fudge
full
fume
fun
fund
funk
funny
fur
further
fuse
fuss
fussy
gag
Gail
gain
gale
gall
galley
gallon
game
gang
garbage
gas
gate
gauze
gave
gaze
gear
gee
geese
gem
gent
gentle
gentleman
gently
George
germ
get
gift
gill
gin
ginger
gingerbread
girl
girlfriend
give
given
glad
glance
gland
glare
glass
gleam
glitter
globe

gloom
gloomy
glove
glow
glue
gnarled
gnash
gnat
gnaw
gnawing
gnome
go
goal
gob
gobble
God
godmother
goes
gold
golden
gold-plated
golly
gone
gong
goo
good
goodness
goods
goof
goofy
goose
gorge
gosh
got
gotten
gown
grab
grace
grade
grain
grand
grandfather
grandmother
grape
grapefruit
grass
grave
graveyard
gray
grease
great
Greece
greed
greedy
Greek
green
greet

grew
grill
grin
grind
grip
gripe
groan
groom
grouch
grouchy
ground
group
grow
growl
grown
grownup
grudge
guard
guess
guest
guide
guilt
guilty
gulf
gull
gully
gulp
gum
gumdrop
gun
gust
gut
gutter
guy
had
hadn't
hail
hair
hairbrush
haircut
hairless
hairpin
hairy
half
hall
halt
ham
hammer
hand
handful
handshake
handwriting
handy
hang
hanger
hangover
happen

happily
happiness
happy
hard
hardly
hardware
harm
harmful
harmless
harp
harsh
Harvey
has
hasn't
hat
hatch
hate
haul
haunt
haunted
have
haven't
hay
he
head
heading
headquarters
health
healthy
hear
heard
heartbeat
heartbreak
heat
heater
heavy
heck
he'd
heel
height
held
helicopter
hell
he'll
hello
help
helper
helpful
helpless
hem
hen
her
herb
Herb
herd
here
herself

he's
hey
hi
hid
hidden
hide
hide-and-seek
hideout
high
high-class
highness
high school
highway
hike
hill
him
himself
hind
hint
hip
hire
his
hiss
hit
hitter
hive
hobby
hock
hoist
hold
holder
holdup
hole
Holly
home
homebody
homeland
homeless
homemade
home run
homesick
homework
homey
honey
honeybee
honk
honor
hood
hook
hop
hope
hopeful
hopeless
horn
horse
horseback
horseplay

hose
hot
hotel
hour
hourglass
hourly
house
household
housewife
housework
how
however
how's
hug
huge
huh
hum
human
hunch
hundred
hung
hunt
hunter
hurl
hurry
hurt
hush
hut
I
ice
ice cream
icing
icy
I'd
idea
if
ill
I'll
I'm
import
important
imported
impose
impress
improper
improperly
improve
impure
in
include
income
increase
index
indoors
infect
infield
inflate

inform
inhale
injure
injury
ink
inland
inquest
inquire
insect
inside
insight
insist
inspire
instead
instruct
intend
intense
intent
into
invade
invent
invite
involve
iron
is
isn't
it
itch
its
it's
I've
ivy
jab
jack
Jack
jacket
jail
jam
January
jar
jaw
jazz
jeans
jeep
jeer
Jello
jelly
jerk
Jerome
Jesus
jet
Jew
Jill
Jim
Joan
job
jobless

John
join
joint
joke
joker
Jones
jot
joy
Joyce
joyful
judge
jug
juice
juicy
July
jump
jumpy
June
junk
jury
just
jut
Kate
keel
keep
keeper
keg
kept
ketchup
key
keyboard
kick
kid
kidnap
kill
kin
kind
kinfolk
king
Kirk
kiss
kit
kitchen
kite
kitty
knack
knapsack
knee
kneecap
knee-deep
kneel
knelt
knew
knickknack
knife
knight
knit

knob	Lee	look	mark	mirror	must	noose
knock	left	loose	Mark	miscount	mute	nope
knockout	leg	loosen	marry	misjudge	my	nor
knot	lemon	lord	Mary	misplace	myself	north
knotty	lend	lose	Martin	miss	nail	Norway
know	lent	loss	mash	misspell	name	nose
known	Lent	lost	mask	mist	nap	nosy
lab	less	lot	mass	mistake	nasty	not
lace	lesson	loud	mat	mistaken	naughty	notch
lack	let	loudly	match	mistreat	near	note
lacy	let's	Louise	matchbook	mistrust	nearby	notebook
lady	letter	lousy	mate	mitt	nearly	nothing
lake	library	love	math	mix	neat	notice
laid	lice	lovely	matter	moan	neatly	November
lamb	lick	lover	Matthew	mob	neck	now
lame	lid	low	may	mock	necktie	nowhere
lamp	lie	lowdown	May	moist	nectar	nude
lance	life	lower	maybe	moisten	need	nudge
land	lifeboat	loyal	Mayflower	mold	needless	numb
landlady	lifeguard	loyally	me	moldy	needy	number
landlord	lifetime	loyalty	meal	mom	neighbor	nurse
landmark	lift	luck	mealtime	moment	neighborhood	nut
landowner	light	luckily	mean	mommy	neither	nutty
lane	lighten	lucky	meaning	Monday	nerve	oak
lap	lighter	lug	meant	money	nervous	oar
lard	lighthouse	Luke	meat	monkey	nest	oat
large	like	lukewarm	meatball	month	net	oatmeal
lark	limb	lump	meatless	mood	never	ocean
last	lime	lunch	meet	moon	new	o'clock
late	limit	lung	meeting	moose	New England	October
lately	limp	lunge	melt	mop	news	odd
later	Linda	lurch	men	mope	newspaper	oddly
laugh	line	machine	mend	more	newsstand	of
laughter	lining	Mack	mention	morning	New Year's Day	off
laundromat	link	mad	merge	most	New Year's Eve	often
laundry	lint	made	mess	motel	New York	oh
law	lip	madly	messy	mother	next	oil
lawful	lipstick	maid	met	mouse	nice	okay
lawn	liquid	mail	mice	mouth	nick	old
lawyer	list	mailbox	middle	mouthful	nickname	on
lay	listen	mailman	middle-aged	move	night	once
lazy	lit	main	midnight	movie	nightclub	one
lead	little	mainly	might	mow	nine	one-celled
leader	live	make	mighty	mower	nineteen	one-half
leaf	lively	maker	Mike	Mr.	ninety	only
leak	living	male	mild	Mrs.	nip	onto
leaky	load	mall	mildly	Ms.	no	ooze
lean	loaf	malt	mile	much	nobody	open
leap	loan	mammal	milk	mud	nod	opposite
leapfrog	lobby	man	million	muddy	noise	or
learn	lock	manager	mince	mug	noisily	order
leash	lodge	mankind	mincemeat	mugger	noisy	other
least	log	Mansfield	mind	mule	none	ouch
leather	lone	many	mine	munch	nonsense	ought
leave	loney	map	miner	murder	nook	ounce
led	long	march	mint	murmur	noon	our
ledge	longing	March	minute	muse	no one	ours

ourselves	park	piggy	popcorn	quarterback	reject	robber
out	part	pigpen	Pope	queen	rejection	robbery
outcome	party	pile	porch	queer	rejoice	robe
outdoors	pass	pill	pork	question	relate	rock
outer	passbook	pillow	port	quick	relax	rocky
outfield	Passover	pin	pot	quickly	remain	rod
outlook	passport	pinch	potato	quiet	remains	rode
outnumber	password	pine	potato chip	quit	remark	role
outside	past	Ping-Pong	pouch	quite	remember	roll
outskirts	paste	pink	pounce	quote	remind	roller
outsmart	pat	Pinocchio	pound	race	remove	Rome
outstanding	patch	pint	pour	rack	renew	roof
oven	path	pipe	pout	raft	rent	room
over	patty	pit	practice	rag	repaid	rope
overall	Paul	pitch	praise	rage	repair	rose
overalls	pause	pitcher	prance	raid	repeat	rosebud
overboard	pave	pitchfork	pray	rail	reply	rosy
overcoat	paving	pity	preach	railroad	report	rot
ovecome	paw	place	preacher	rain	reporter	rotten
overdone	pawn	plain	present	rainbow	request	rough
overdraw	pay	plainly	president	rainy	require	round
overflow	paycheck	plan	press	raise	respect	route
overgrown	payday	plane	pretty	rake	respond	row
overhead	payment	plant	pretzel	ram	rest	rowboat
overlook	pea	plate	price	ramp	restless	Roy
overnight	peace	platter	pride	ran	restroom	royal
overseas	peaceful	play	prince	rang	retire	royally
overtime	peacefully	player	print	range	retreat	royalty
overweight	peach	playground	prize	rank	return	rub
owe	peanut	plea	probably	rare	reveal	rubber
own	pear	plead	problem	rarely	revive	rude
owner	peck	pleasant	proof	rash	rhyme	rug
ox	peek	please	prop	rat	rib	rule
pace	peel	pleased	proper	rate	rice	ruler
pack	peeler	pledge	properly	raw	rich	run
pact	peep	plenty	property	reach	rid	rung
pad	peer	plot	proud	react	ridden	runny
padding	pen	plow	proudly	read	ride	runt
page	penny	plug	prune	reading	ridge	rush
paid	people	plum	pry	ready	rig	rust
pail	pep	plump	pub	real	right	rut
pain	pepper	plunge	puff	really	rim	Ruth
painful	perch	plus	puffy	rear	ring	sack
painless	period	poach	pull	reason	ringside	sad
paint	perk	pod	pulse	recall	rinse	sadly
paintbrush	person	point	pump	recipe	rip	sadness
painter	pest	poke	punch	record	ripe	safe
painting	pet	poker	punk	recover	rise	safely
pair	phone	pole	punt	recovery	risen	said
pale	phony	police	purr	red	risk	sail
palm	piano	policeman	purse	reduce	risky	sailor
pan	pick	pond	push	reel	river	sake
pancake	pickle	pool	put	reform	road	sale
pane	picture	poor	putty	refresh	roadwork	salesman
pant	pie	poorhouse	quack	refrigerator	roar	salt
pants	piece	poorly	quart	refund	roast	salty
paper	pig	pop	quarter	refuse	rob	Sam

same season shopper sixty smell sound spy
sample seat shopping size smile soundly square
sand seaweed shore skate Smith soup squarely
sandwich second short skater smog sour squeak
sang see shortcake sketch smoke sourball squeaky
sank seed shorts ski smoker sourpuss squeal
sat seek shortstop skid smoky south squeeze
Saturday seem shot skill smooth space squirm
sauce seen shotgun skillful smoothly spaghetti squirrel
saucepan seep should skin smudge Spain squirt
saucer self shoulder skinny snack span stage
save sell shouldn't skip snag spangle stagecoach
savings send shout skirt snail spank stage fright
saw sense shove skull snake spare stain
say sent show skunk snap spark stair
saying sentence shower sky snappy speak stairway
says September showoff slacks snapshot speaker stale
scald serve shown slam snarl spear stall
scale set shrank slang snatch speck stamp
scar seven shrill slant sneak sped stand
scare seventeen shrimp slap sneakers speech standstill
scarecrow seventh shrink slaughter sneaky speed star
scarf seventy shrug slave sneeze spell starch
scheme sex shrunk sled sniff spend stare
school shack shut sleep snip spendthrift starfish
scold shade shy sleepily snob spent start
scoop shady shyly sleepless snore spice starve
scorch shake sick sleepy snow spicy stash
score shaken side sleet snowball spill state
scoreboard shaky side show sleeve snowplow spin station
scotch shame sidewalk sleeveless snowstorm spine stay
Scotch shape sideways sleigh so spit steak
Scott share sift slept soak spite steam
scour shark sigh slice soap spiteful steel
scout sharp sight slid soar splash steep
scram sharply sign slide sob spleen stem
scrap shatter silent slight sock splint step
scrape shave silk slim socks splinter Steve
scraper she sill sling soft split Steven
scratch she'd silly slip softly splurge stew
scratchy sheep simple slipper soil spoke stick
scream sheer sin slot sold spoken sticker
screech sheet since slouch sole spoil sticky
screen shelf sinful slow solid spoon still
screw shell sing slowdown some spoonful sting
scribe shelter singe slowly somebody sponge stink
script she's singer slowpoke someone sport stir
scroll shift single slum something spot stitch
scrounge shine sink slump sometimes spotless stocking
scrub shiny sip slung somewhat spout stone
scruff ship sir slush son sprain stony
sea shipwreck sister sly song sprawl stood
seacoast shirt sit smack soon spray stool
seafood shock sitter small sore spread stoop
seal shook six smart sorry spring stop
seaport shoot six-shooter smash sort sprint store
search shop sixteen smear sought sprout stork

storm
story
stove
straight
straighten
strain
strand
strange
stranger
strap
straw
stray
streak
stream
streamline
street
stress
stressful
stretch
strict
strike
string
strip
stripe
stroke
strong
strongly
struck
struggle
stuck
study
stuff
stuffing
stuffy
stunt
stutter
sub
subject
subway
success
successful
successfully
such
suck
suds
sue
Sue
sugar
sugarless
suit
suitcase
sulk
sulky
sum
summer
sun
sunburn

Sunday
sundown
sung
sunglasses
sunk
sunken
sunless
sunlight
sunny
sunrise
sunshine
suppose
sure
surely
surf
surprise
Sutter
swam
swear
sweat
sweater
Swede
Sweden
sweep
sweeper
sweet
swell
swept
swift
swiftly
swim
swimmer
swing
swipe
Swiss
switch
swizzle
sworn
swung
syllable
tab
table
tablecloth
tablespoon
tack
tag
tail
tailor
tailspin
take
taken
tale
talk
tall
tame
tan
tank

tap
tape
tar
task
taste
tasteless
tasty
taught
tax
tea
teach
teacher
teacup
team
teapot
tear
tearoom
tease
teaspoon
Ted
tee
teepee
teeth
television
tell
teller
temper
temperature
ten
tend
tense
tent
term
test
than
thank
thankful
Thanksgiving
that
that's
thaw
the
theft
their
them
themselves
then
there
there's
these
they
they're
thick
thickly
thief
thin
thinner

thing
think
thinker
third
thirst
thirsty
thirteen
thirty
this
thorn
those
though
thought
thoughtful
thoughtless
thousand
thread
threat
threaten
three
threw
thrift
thrifty
thrill
throat
throb
throne
through
throughout
throw
thrown
thud
thumb
thump
Thursday
thus
tick
tide
tie
tight
tighten
tightly
tile
tilt
Tim
time
tin
tip
tire
to
toast
toaster
today
together
toil
told
Tom

tomato
tomorrow
ton
tone
tonight
Tony
too
took
tool
toolbox
tooth
toothbrush
toothpaste
top
tore
torn
toss
touch
touchdown
tough
toward
towel
town
townspeople
toy
trace
track
trade
trail
train
trainer
tramp
trance
trap
trapper
trash
trashy
tray
tread
treat
tree
trend
tribe
trick
tricky
trim
trip
troop
trooper
trouble
trounce
trousers
trout
truce
truck
trudge
true

trunk
trust
truth
thruthful
truthfully
try
tub
tube
tuck
Tuesday
tug
tune
turn
twelve
twenty
twice
twin
twine
twist
two
ugly
ulcer
unable
unafraid
unarmed
uncertain
unclear
uncooked
uncover
under
underdog
underdone
underground
underline
underneath
undershirt
understand
understood
undertaker
underwear
underworld
undid
undo
undress
uneasy
uneven
unfair
unfit
unfold
unfriendly
unhappy
unhealthy
unit
United States
universe
unlawful
unless

unlikely
unlucky
unmade
unmated
unpack
unpaid
unsafe
untie
until
untrained
unwilling
unwrap
up
up-and-down
upcoming
update
uphill
upkeep
upon
uproar
upset
upside-down
upstairs
upstate
uptown
us
use
useful
useless
utter
van
vane
vanilla
vase
veal
verge
verse
very
vest
vice
vine
visit
voice
void
volt
vote
voter
vow
vowel
wade
wage
waist
waistline
wait
waiter
wake
walk

wall
wallet
Walter
waltz
wander
want
war
warm
warm-blooded
warn
warning
was
wash
washbowl
washcloth
washing
Washington
wasn't
waste
wastebasket
wasteful
watch
watchful
watchman
water
watery
wave
wavy
wax
way
we
weak
weaken
wear
weather
web
wed
wedding
Wednesday
weed
week
weekday
weekend
weekly
weep
weigh
weight
well
we'll
well-done
well-known
went
were
we're
weren't
west
wet

whack
whale
wham
what
whatever
what's
whatsoever
wheat
wheel
wheeze
when
whenever
where
wherever
whether
which
whichever
whiff
while
whim
whine
whip
whirl
white
who
whoever
whole
whom
who's
whose
why
wide
widespread
wife
wig
wild
wildflower
wildly
will
William
willing
wilt
win
window
wine
wing
wink
winner
winter
wipe
wire
wiring
wiry
wise
wisecrack
wisely
wish

witch
with
within
without
woke
woman
women
won
wonder
won't
wood
woodpecker
woodwork
woody
wool
wolly
word
wore
work
worker
workshop
world
worm
worn
worse
worst
worth
worthless
worthy
would
wouldn't
wound
wow
wrap
wrapper
wrapping
wreck
wrecker
wren
wrench
wring
wrist
wristwatch
write
writer
writing
written
wrong
wrote
wrung
yard
yawn
ye
yeah
year
yearly
yell

yes
yesterday
yet
Y.M.C.A.
yoga
yogurt
yolk
you
you'd
you'll
young
your
you're
yourself
you've
yuk!
Yule
zip
zipper
zone
zoo